C000292531

St Margaret's Gospel-book

St Margaret's

The favourite book of an eleventh-century Queen of Scots

Gospel-book

REBECCA RUSHFORTH

BODLEIAN LIBRARY
UNIVERSITY OF OXFORD

TREASURES FROM THE BODLEIAN LIBRARY

The Bodleian Library, founded in 1602, is the principal library of the University of Oxford and one of the world's great libraries. Over the past four hundred years, the Library has built up an outstanding collection of manuscripts and rare books which make up part of our common cultural heritage. Each title in this lavishly-illustrated series, Treasures from the Bodleian Library, explores the intellectual and artistic value of a single witness of human achievement, within the covers of one book. Overall, the series aims to promote knowledge and to contribute to our understanding and enjoyment of the Library's collections across a range of disciplines and subjects.

First published in 2007 by the Bodleian Library
Broad Street
Oxford OX1 3BG

www.bodleianbookshop.co.uk

ISBN: 185124 370 4
ISBN 13: 978 1 85124 370 4

Text © Rebecca Rushforth, 2007
Images © Bodleian Library, University of Oxford, and other named copyright holders, 2007

Designed by Baseline Arts, Ltd
Series design by Dot Little
Typeset in Monotype Centaur
Printed and bound by The University Press, Cambridge
British Library Catalogue in Publishing Data
A CIP record of this publication is available from the British Library

Contents

INCIPIT EVAN
GELIVM SCDM
MATHEVM.

LIBER

GENE

RATIO

nis ihu xpi filii dauid. filii
Abraham. Abraham autem ge
nuit isaac. isaac autem genuit ia
cob. Iacob autem genuit iudam
& fratres eius. iudas autem genuit
phares & zara dethamar. Phares
autem genuit esrom. esrom aut
genuit aram.

Preface

I have drawn heavily on work mentioned in the further reading section, especially that of Richard Gameson and Lois Huneycutt. Translations draw on those cited in the further reading section, but have usually been adapted according to my own understanding. I must record my gratitude for the generous help of a number of people: Samuel Fanous; Emily Joliffe; Simon Keynes; Martin Kauffmann; Peter Kidd; Adrian Joyce; James Lawson; Tim Harris; Laura Hill; Sally Devlin; the nuns of St Mary's Abbey, West Malling, Kent; the monks of the Abbaye Notre Dame du Bec, Le Bec-Hellouin, Normandy; the Master and Fellows of Corpus Christi College, Cambridge; Keith and Heather Rushforth; Timothy Rushforth; Kitty Rushforth; Bruce Barker-Benfield; Patricia Aske; Gill Cannell; Godfrey Waller; Nigel Morgan; Timofey Guimon; Richard Gameson; Julian Harrison; and Cynthia Harper.

I would like to dedicate this book to Heather Rushforth, my mother, who is always a good example.

FIGURE I
The start of the Gospel
of St John from St
Margaret's Gospel-book.
Oxford, Bodleian Library, MS.
Lat. liturg. f. 5, 30v–31r

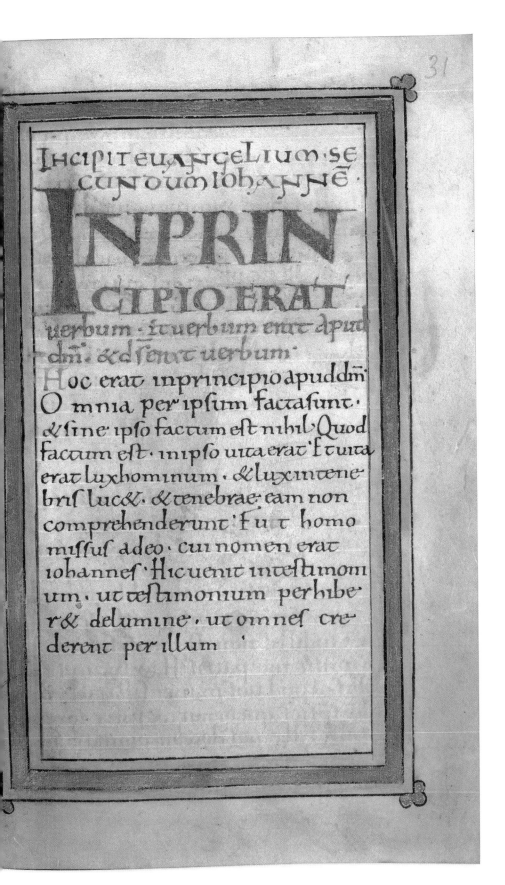

INCIPIT EUANGELIUM SE
CUNDUM IOHANNE.

INPRIN
CIPIO ERAT
uerbum. et uerbum erat apud
dm. & ds erat uerbum.
Hoc erat inprincipio apud dm.
Omnia per ipsum facta sunt.
& sine ipso factum est nihil. Quod
factum est. in ipso uita erat. Et uita
erat lux hominum. & lux in tene
bris lucet. & tenebrae eam non
comprehenderunt. Fuit homo
missus adeo. cui nomen erat
iohannes. Hic uenit intestimoni
um. ut testimonium perhibe
r& delumine. ut omnes cre
derent per illum.

Introduction

THE LIFE OF St Margaret, eleventh-century queen of Scotland, was affected by many political upheavals; although forced into an unwelcome public role, she became famous for her piety, dignity and compassion. After her death she was invoked as an image of stability and reconciliation in England and Scotland, even as late as the Restoration of Charles II. Her favourite book, an illuminated manuscript of extracts from the Gospels, survives in the Bodleian Library at Oxford.

Although Margaret was later revered as a saint, her Latin biographer, Turgot, recounts only a single miracle, an occasion on which this very Gospel-book was preserved from damage:

> *She had a Gospel-book, covered all over with jewels and gold, in which pictures of the four evangelists were embellished with paint mixed with gold, and all the way through it each capital letter glowed red-gold. She had always loved this book more dearly than the other ones she studied and read. Once, when the book was travelling with her, it happened that she crossed a ford, and the book, which had been carelessly wrapped in cloths, fell in the river. The person who had been carrying the book continued to ride along, unconcerned because he had no idea that he had dropped it. Indeed it was some time later, when he went to get the book out, that he first realised it was not there. For a long time it was sought but not found.*
>
> *At length the book was discovered, lying open at the bottom of a deep river, its pages constantly swept back and forth by the rapid motion of the water. It had had some little silk cloths to protect the golden letters from contact with the facing pages, but these cloths had been swept away by the force of the river. Who would think that the book was worth anything any longer? Who would believe that even one letter would still appear in it? But without a doubt, it was drawn up from the middle of the river intact, incorrupt, and undamaged, so much so that it scarcely seemed to have been touched by the water! The pages were as white as before, and everything was intact, and the forms of the letters remained just as they had been. The only damage was to the end leaves, where some signs of moisture could just barely be seen. At once, the book was brought back to the queen, and the miracle related to her, and she gave thanks to Christ; and from then on the queen loved the book even more than she had before.*

FIGURE 2
An early twentieth-century
stained-glass window in
St Margaret's Chapel, Edinburgh.

FIGURE 3

The page with the added poem: note that the scribe started to write the text continuously as if it were prose, but then switched to writing one line of poetry, or hexameter, per line of the page. The handwriting is generically similar to that of the main book, but some features point to its later date. To judge from the script, which is of a very late Anglo-Saxon type, the poem was probably written into the book towards the end of the eleventh century or at the start of the twelfth; the way in which it refers to the king and queen suggests they were still alive, which would date its addition before 1093. References to 'this book', *hunc librum*, show that the poem was composed specifically to be written into the manuscript.

Oxford, Bodleian Library, MS. Lat. liturg. f. 5, 2r

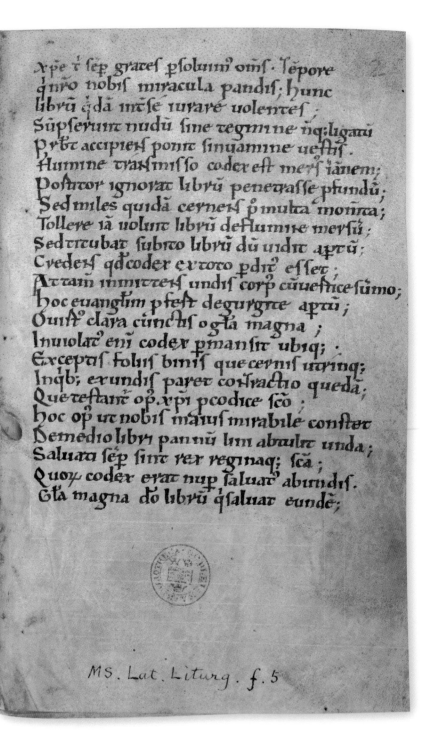

bat inficiendo · illinc pagan̄ q̄m detesta
bile ſit in humana p̄sumere ſup̄bia expi̅t
cadendo; hoc itaq; p̄lio abſq; detrim̄to
ſui exerc̄it c̄fecto: elfredus totī brittan
nie ip̄iu obtinuit · & q̄m ſc̄i c̄fessoriſ
p̄cepta que ſuſcepat inpenuria · memo
rit̄ ſeruabat in curia: om̄ib; ſep̄er &
ubique aduerſ ſanctū p̄ualuit molim̄inib;

·l· Quoin̄ tempeſtate orta treſ und̄e inna
uī in qua corpuſ eiuſ abducebat̄ cadentes
in ſanguinem conuerteb̄antur ·

FIGURE 4
The story of the miraculous
preservation of Margaret's
Gospel-book is paralleled by
stories of other saints' books.
This twelfth-century manuscript
relates how when the monks of
Lindisfarne had been driven from
their island home by Viking
attacks, they tried to take
Cuthbert's body with them to
seek refuge in Ireland, the
spiritual home of their founders.
A violent storm rose up and
overwhelmed their ship, washing
overboard the Gospels of St
Cuthbert, and forcing the monks
to turn back. The Gospel-book
was probably the Lindisfarne
Gospels now in the British
Library. Cuthbert himself
appeared in a vision to one of
the monks to direct them to
where the manuscript had washed
up on the foreshore; they found
it miraculously unscathed by the
ordeal.[1]

Oxford, University College, MS. 165, p. 143

Now, people should decide for themselves what they think about this; I myself consider it a sign from God of his esteem for the venerable queen.[1]

A Latin poem added to the beginning of the Bodleian Gospel-book describes the same events:

Ever to you, O Christ, we render thanks
who shows us miracles in our own time!
Some people who took this book to swear an oath
carried it off uncovered and unfastened;
a priest conveyed it tucked into his robes.
Crossing a river, the bearer unaware,
the book fell in the torrent, pierced the depths.
A soldier some time later saw it there
and wanted at once to pull it from the flow;
but faltered when he saw the book was open,
thinking that it would be completely ruined.
But still, head-first he dived into the rapids
and fetched the Gospel open from the gulf.
O virtue clear to all! O, great glory!
For, the whole book remained immaculate
except for the two leaves seen at either end
which, buckled by the waves' effect, proclaim
Christ's intervention for the holy book.
That this should seem to us more marvellous
the waves had washed a cloth out of the centre.
May ever the king and holy queen be well
whose book was lately rescued from the waves!
All glory be to God who saved this book![2]

The close correspondence of the story in Margaret's *Life* and the events of the poem make it clear that we have in this little manuscript St Margaret's own favourite book.[3]

Similar stories are told of some other medieval manuscripts. The Lindisfarne Gospels are said to have been protected by St Cuthbert when they fell in the sea, and in legend the books of St Patrick and St Columba were also invulnerable to water damage.[4] When he tells this story about Margaret's Gospel-book, her biographer links her to venerable figures from the Insular and Gaelic past. Her connection to the English past was more immediately apparent.

Who was Margaret?

IN 1046, WHEN Margaret was born, her father Edward was by birth the closest heir to the throne of Anglo-Saxon England; but he had been compelled to leave his native land long before this, and is known to history as Edward the Exile (*see Family Tree, p.106*). Through him Margaret was directly descended from King Alfred the Great; she traced her ancestry back from Alfred via Woden and Noah to Adam (as indeed, via St Margaret, could our current queen).

The story of Edward's exile and his claim to the Anglo-Saxon throne starts at the end of the tenth century, before his birth. The rich lands of England were always a tempting target for Viking raiders; in 991 at Maldon in Essex the English general, Byrhtnoth, was killed in battle, and the Vikings gained possession of the field. This led to the first payment of the *Danegeld*, a tribute which it was hoped would induce them to go away and leave the English in peace. But the Vikings were not a single group, and agreements made with one band were not necessarily respected by others; runic inscriptions in Scandinavia and coin hoards full of English pennies attest to how Viking men could make their fortune through raids on England at this time. Increasing sums of money were needed to pay them off, and the *Anglo-Saxon Chronicle*'s tale of the English defence is a litany of incompetence and treachery. The king of England, Æthelred, is known to history as 'the Unready', meaning bad counsel or no counsel (a pun on his name which means noble counsel), and throughout his reign he was plagued by ambitious and untrustworthy nobles. The Vikings, meeting so little resistance, turned their thoughts from raiding to conquest, and more systematic attacks occurred. In 1014 the Danish leader Swein took control of much of England. In 1016, after the deaths of Æthelred and Swein, England was split between their respective sons, Edmund Ironside and Cnut. However, Edmund Ironside died later that same year, and the young Cnut, barely out of his teens, became king of all England. The Danish Conquest was complete.

FIGURE 5
The only English king known by the epithet 'Great', Alfred (871–99) was not only a remarkable military leader who brought England back from the brink of total conquest by the Vikings, but also a learned man concerned with educational and religious reforms. He set in motion a programme of translating important Christian Latin texts into English to make them more readily available, and did some of the work of translation himself. This jewel has an inscription on it saying that Alfred had it made. As part of his programme of educational reforms we know that he had copies of his translations sent out to bishops' each accompanied by a valuable 'æstel'. No one knows for certain what an 'æstel' is but it was probably a kind of pointer to move along the lines while reading, and this jewel may have been the decorated top of one such 'æstel'.[5]

The Alfred Jewel, Ashmolean Museum, Oxford

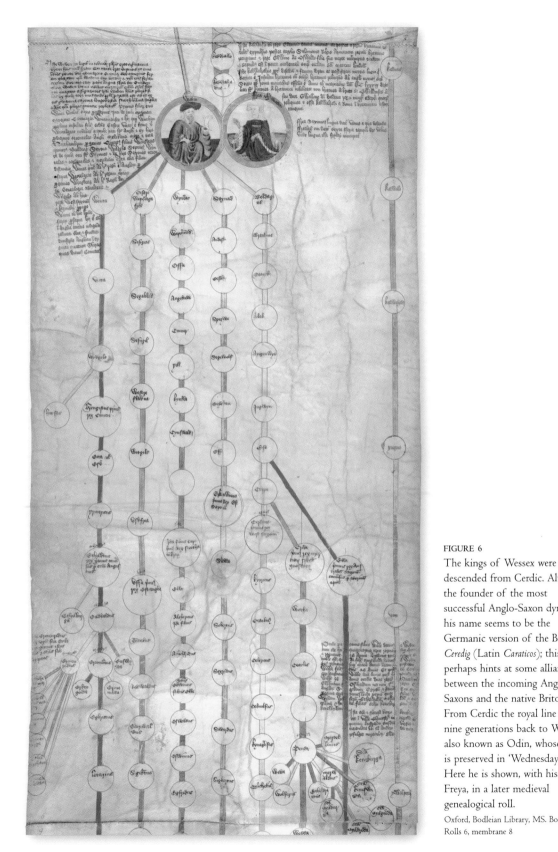

FIGURE 6

The kings of Wessex were descended from Cerdic. Although the founder of the most successful Anglo-Saxon dynasty, his name seems to be the Germanic version of the British *Ceredig* (Latin *Caraticos*); this perhaps hints at some alliance between the incoming Anglo-Saxons and the native Britons.[6] From Cerdic the royal line traced nine generations back to Woden, also known as Odin, whose name is preserved in 'Wednesday'. Here he is shown, with his 'wife' Freya, in a later medieval genealogical roll.

Oxford, Bodleian Library, MS. Bodley Rolls 6, membrane 8

Cnut was later to be remembered as a model Christian king, law-respecting and generous to the church, but before he could embark on this way of life he had to tie up some dynastic loose ends: Cnut either killed or exiled all of Æthelred's surviving sons, and married Æthelred's widowed queen, Emma of Normandy. Edmund Ironside had married a certain Ealdgyth, a well-connected widow, in 1015 and he left two sons by her, possibly twins, at least one of whom must have been born after Edmund's death. These babies posed a potential threat to Cnut's rule, but he baulked at murdering them. Instead he sent them to the king of Sweden to be killed far from English eyes. The king declined to do this but could not harbour them for political reasons; the children grew up in exile at a series of Eastern European courts, probably including Kievan Russia. One of the boys, Edmund, did not survive, but the other, Edward the Exile, lived to marry a woman called Agatha, a relative of Henry II, Holy Roman Emperor. Although we know very little about the events of Edward's exile, his royal birth must have been respected for him to have made such a prominent marriage.

Meanwhile, back in England the throne passed from Cnut to his sons Harold Harefoot and Harthacnut. Harthacnut's mother was the same Emma of Normandy who had been married first to Æthelred the Unready. It was probably due to her influence that the young Harthacnut, perhaps knowing he was unwell, recalled his older half-brother Edward the Confessor from his long exile in Normandy to be his heir. Later it was seen as a sign of Edward's sanctity that he had regained his ancestral throne against such odds, and without the need for warfare. But when Harthacnut died childless in 1042, aged only about twenty-four, Edward was not the only claimant to the throne; Cnut's family provided other heirs among the royalty of Scandinavia. Edward may have pacified the Scandinavian claim with promises about the succession should he die childless. Furthermore, it was clear that he could not remain king without the support of the English earls, in particular the powerful Godwin and his family. Probably at around the same time that Edward the Exile married Agatha, his uncle Edward the Confessor married Godwin's daughter Edith, but no children were born of the match.

From quite early on in the reign of Edward the Confessor it was clear that the succession was going to be a big issue: the king may have dangled the possibility of being his heir before various parties as a political bargaining point, but the throne was not entirely his to give away, and the English earls wanted an English heir. Edith and Edward's lack of children left Edward without a clear successor; as a consequence the sons of Edmund Ironside were recalled, although it took some years for them to be traced. In the spring of 1057 Edward the Exile arrived in England with his wife Agatha and his children Margaret, Christina, and Edgar. On the 19 April he died without even meeting his uncle the king. He had left England probably within a year of his birth and died within weeks of his return. The *Anglo-Saxon Chronicle*

laments, 'I do not know why it was not allowed that he should meet his uncle': this has been interpreted as suggesting some sort of foul play, but probably it is simply a lament for the inexorable ways of fate. The Exile's family remained in England: Agatha, Margaret, and Christina were probably under the protection of Edith, Edward's queen. Edgar became known as the Ætheling, meaning prince or heir, but he was only about five years old at the time of his father's death, and Edward the Confessor was already in his fifties, older than any previous king of his line.

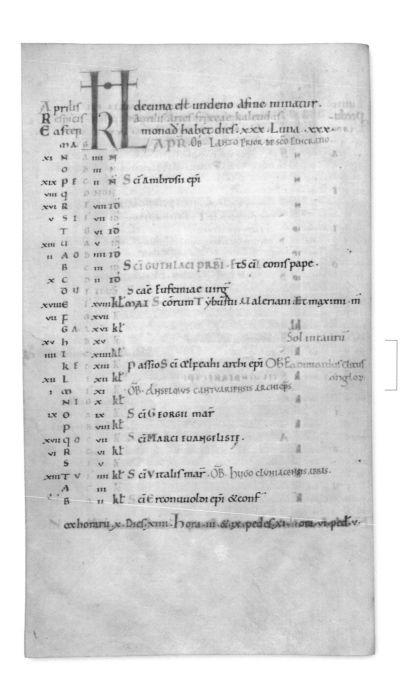

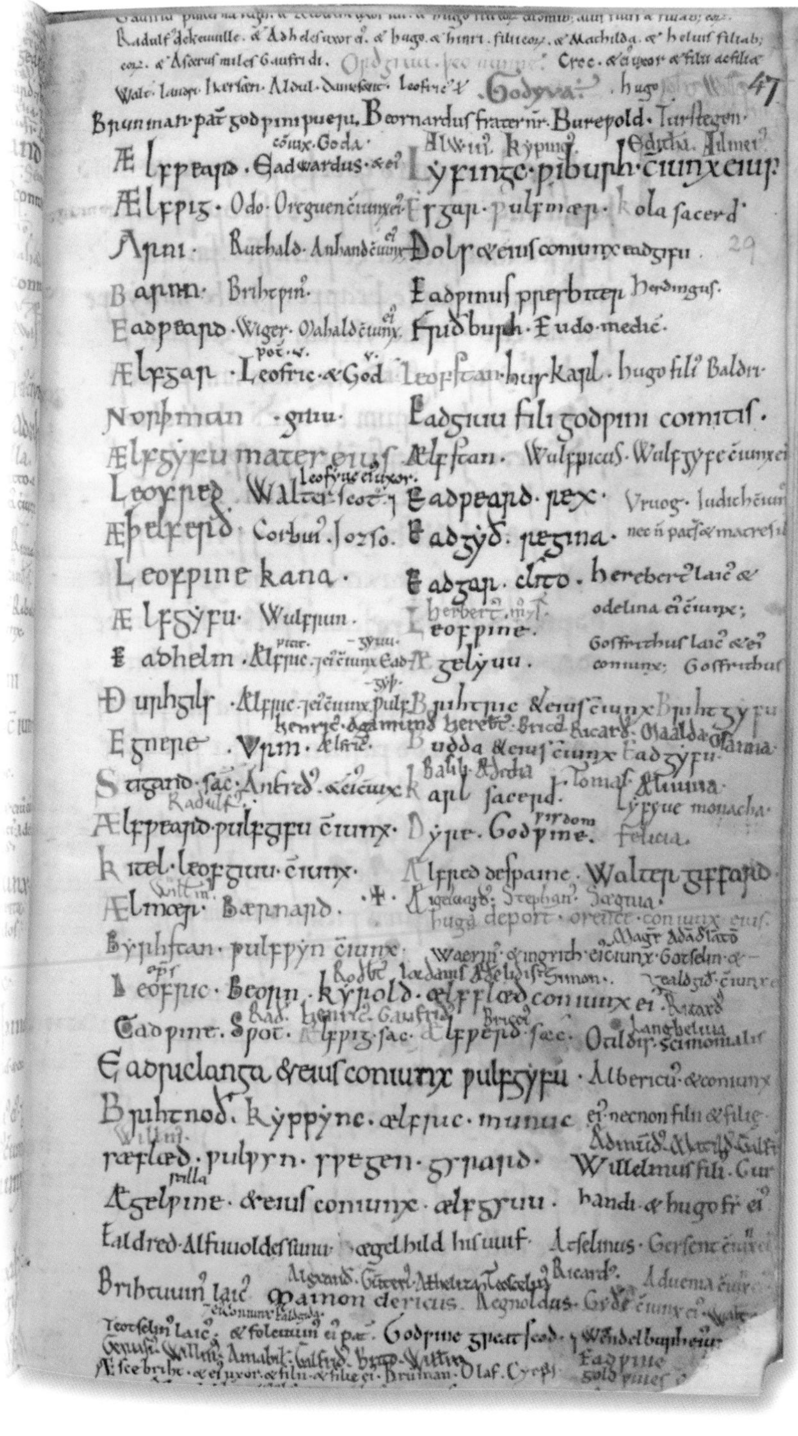

FIGURE 9

Sometime in the late 1050s or first half of the 1060s the royal family visited the New Minster at Winchester. This monastery had been founded under the encouragement of King Edgar the Peacemaker in the 960s, and had always had close links with the monarchy. From the 1030s the monastery kept a *Liber vitae*, or book of life, in which they wrote the names of people who were friends of the monastery, and whom they remembered in their prayers. This picture shows the names of Edward, his wife Edith, and Edgar the Ætheling, written in the book; Edgar is called *clito*, a Latin word for *ætheling* or prince, showing that he was the designated heir. His importance is emphasized by the fact that only these three names, Edward, Edith, and Edgar, were written into the book at the same time. It is interesting that Edward the Confessor's name had not been added to the confraternity book before this point; possibly this was because Ælfwine, abbot of the New Minster from 1031 to 1057, had had close links with the intermediate Danish dynasty of Cnut.[7]

London, British Library, MS. Stowe 944, 29r

Margaret and the Norman Conquest

The ruler-portrait on a coin of Edward the Confessor. In the Middle Ages there were three main types of saint: martyrs, who died for their faith; confessors, men who led a very holy life and provided inspiration for others; and virgins, almost always female, who were celebrated for their sexual purity. Edward was called the Confessor because he was held to have lived an unusually good life, and he was revered as a saint from not long after his death. His childlessness, which caused trouble for the succession of the throne, was believed to result from a chaste marriage to Edith, Harold's sister, whom he was said to have treated more like a daughter than a wife.[8] The epithet Confessor distinguishes this Edward from his murdered uncle, King Edward the Martyr.

Coin of Edward the Confessor, Ashmolean Museum, Oxford

A T CHRISTMAS 1065 Edward the Confessor was too ill to attend the consecration of Westminster Abbey, his own much-prized foundation; within a fortnight he was buried there. The succession was unclear. Edgar the Ætheling was the only surviving descendant of Æthelred in the male line and had the best blood claim: but he was inexperienced, no more than fourteen years old. Invasions were likely from both north and south; now was not the time for a young and untested king. Instead Edward was succeeded by his brother-in-law Harold Godwinsson, the most powerful of the earls, to whom Edward seems to have offered the crown on his deathbed.

England was now threatened from opposite directions by two overseas rulers who each felt they had a right to the English throne. Harald Hardrada, king of Norway, was in some sense an heir of Cnut in Scandinavia. It was believed by many that Harthacnut had promised Magnus, king of Norway, the throne of England should he die childless. Harthacnut's childless death instead resulted in the succession of Edward the Confessor, but it is possible that Edward had pacified the Scandinavian claim with similar promises, and Harald Hardrada was Magnus's heir. He was the brother of St Olaf, king of Norway, and was with him when he was 'martyred' in 1030; St Olaf was already widely revered in England before 1066.

Harald had a formidable international reputation as a fighter and ruler. He had seen service as head of the elite Varangian Guard in Byzantium, where he had been involved in the deposition of an Emperor; he had led raids on Muslim Africa and Sicily; he had spent time in the court of King Jaroslav of Novogorod, and had succeeded to the Norwegian throne in 1047. Harald Hardrada united with Tostig, Harold II's brother, who had been driven from his Northumbrian earldom in 1065 in a local rebellion. Together they landed with a significant force in the north of England in September 1066. Harold II apparently had no advance warning of this invasion, but he and his army travelled with impressive speed to meet the invaders; and on 25

September defeated them at the Battle of Stamford Bridge. Harald Hardrada and Tostig were both killed.

Harold had overcome the Scandinavian threat. But on the very next day, 26 September, another invasion fleet set sail. William of Normandy was the illegitimate son of Edward the Confessor's mother's nephew; however, this very weak blood-connection to the English throne was strengthened by his claim of two separate promises. Edward the Confessor had taken refuge in Normandy as a youth when Cnut became king of England; and he is supposed to have promised the throne to William in 1051 during a brief period of rebellion against the power of the Godwin family (*see Family Tree, p.106*), perhaps in the hope of gaining assistance against them. However, the Godwins were quickly restored, and by 1057 Edward was instead seeking an heir from among his paternal kin in the form of Edward the Exile. In 1064 or 1065 Harold crossed the channel and fell briefly into the power of William, probably while trying to negotiate the release of a brother and nephew who had been given to William as hostages by Edward the Confessor in 1051; the Normans claimed that at this point Harold made a vow of fealty to William which made him an oath-breaker when he took the English throne.

The arrival of the Norman invaders at Pevensey on 28 September 1066 necessitated a fast turnaround for the victors of Stamford Bridge. While the Normans ravaged the Kentish countryside, the English army marched down to meet them, joining battle at Hastings on 14 October 1066. The result was a devastating defeat for the English, who lost not only their king, but his brothers the earls Leofwine and Gyrth, and much of the English nobility.

Edgar the Ætheling was now chosen as king by the *witan*, the king's council who theoretically had the right to choose every Anglo-Saxon king; but by Christmas he had submitted to William the Conqueror. He was young and inexperienced, with no powerful kinsmen to support him.

Despite his later harsh actions in crushing rebellion, particularly in the famous 'harrying of the North', William was at first a conciliatory leader who sought to rule with the agreement of the surviving English nobles. He allowed Edgar and his family their freedom.

In around 1068 Agatha, Margaret, Christina, and Edgar embarked on a ship and fled England; they landed on the coast of Scotland. Whether or not this was intentional — some accounts hold that Agatha intended to return the family to Hungary but was blown off course — the Scottish court was a good place of asylum for the political exiles. The Scottish king, Máel Coluim or Malcolm (often known as Canmore), had himself been driven from Scotland as a youth after the death of his father King Duncan.

Malcolm had taken refuge in England, at the court of his uncle Siward, the powerful earl of York. In 1057 Edward the Confessor authorized Earl Siward to undertake an invasion of Scotland in Malcolm's favour, and

FIGURE 12 *right*
This illustration of the Battle of Hastings from a fifteenth-century manuscript is filled with anachronisms: the participants wear late medieval armour and have coats of arms. But in a way this is appropriate because this battle was seen to have had a long-lasting importance in English life.
Oxford, Bodleian Library, MS. Laud misc. 733, 70v

hanne this bataile was thus done and duke Willm
Bastard hadde conquered all englond, atte cristes
masse than nept folowyng, he lete coroune hym
kyng atte westmynstre And he conquered þe lande
wel and wysely And he pafe curtesly to his knyghtes þt were
wyth hym of englissh men landes and rentes And whan he
had so done, he wente over the see into Normandie and there
he dwelles a litil while, And in the secound pere of his regne
he come apen into Englond and brought wyth hym Maude
his wyfe and made hire quene of Englond vpon Whit sonday
And anone ther after Mancoloun that was kyng of Scot
lande bygan forto werre vpon duke Willm And duke W.
ordeyned hym in all that he myght bothe by lande & by water

Malcolm features in Shakespeare's Scottish play as the rightful heir to the throne of Scotland, usurped by MacBeth, his father's murderer. In fact things were more complex than this: the Scottish kingship did not automatically pass from father to son; Duncan, who was not an old man, was not murdered but killed in battle; and MacBeth was from another line with a good claim to the throne. MacBeth was perhaps the last king of Scotland in the true Gaelic style; after him the rulers were usually heavily influenced by England or the continent. From the reign of Margaret's son David it became customary for the heir of Scotland to hold extensive lands in the east of England, and to do fealty to the English king for them.

Malcolm kneeling before Edward the Confessor, from Frank Howard, *The Spirit of the Plays of Shakespeare* (London, 1827)

Malcolm: *Be't their comfort*
   We are coming thither: gracious
      England hath
   Lent us good Siward and ten
      thousand men;
   An older and a better soldier none
   That Christendom gives out.
      Macbeth, *Act IV scene iii*

FIGURE 14 *below*
The record of the marriage of Malcolm and Margaret in the Peterborough version of the *Anglo-Saxon Chronicle.*

Oxford, Bodleian Library, MS. Laud misc. 636, 58r

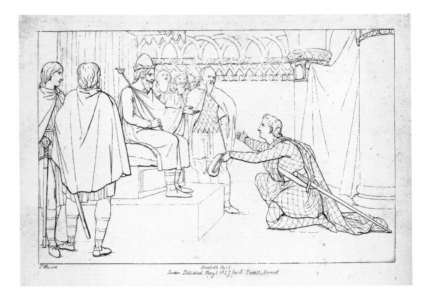

MacBeth, who had succeeded Malcolm's father Duncan, was killed. After Malcolm had secured the Scottish throne in the following year he had maintained close links with England: in 1059 he had travelled to Edward the Confessor's court, where he may have met Edgar the Ætheling and his sisters; and in 1065 he had harboured Earl Tostig, Siward's successor. By the time the Ætheling and his family arrived in Scotland there were probably already many Anglo-Saxon exiles there.

Margaret, we are told both by her biographer and by the *Anglo-Saxon Chronicle*, had intended to become a nun, and vowed her life to God. However Malcolm's first wife, the Scandinavian Ingebjørg, mother of his two sons, had either died or left him by this point, and Malcolm proposed to marry Margaret. The young Edgar, as the *Chronicle* tells us, was eventually persuaded to consent to Malcolm's request, although Margaret was unwilling: 'indeed he dared not do anything else, because they had come into his control'. Because of the Danish Conquest Margaret had been born in exile; as a child political machinations over Edward's successor had dragged her and her family from the far side of Europe and left her orphaned in a strange land; now the Norman Conquest led to another change of country, and an unwelcome marriage. Yet she adapted to this situation to become a much-loved and revered ruler, and a committed wife and mother, renowned even overseas for her goodness and charity.

MARGARET'S GOSPEL-BOOK
Making the Book
When Margaret's Gospel-book was made, in the middle of the eleventh century, a series of complex crafts was required to construct a book. Book-production at this time was centred in the monasteries, where books were most needed. Nonetheless we know that lay people, as well as monks and nuns, made books, and there is evidence that a well-off individual could order a book to be made for their private use or to give away. Margaret may have commissioned the manuscript or bought it second-hand, or she could have been given it as a present.

Parchment
The process of making a book started with preparing a surface to write on. Paper was not used in England at this time — the first English paper mill was not set up until the thirteenth century — and books were instead written on parchment made from animal skins. The person who made the parchment for Margaret's Gospel-book, a monk or nun or perhaps a lay craftsman, would have started with the skin of a calf. (The book seems to be written on calfskin, but it is not easy to tell, and it is possible that sheepskin or even some other animal skin was used.) He or she then soaked it in a caustic liquid, perhaps involving stale urine, and scraped it to take off the hairs and any remaining fleshy tissues. So far this was much the same process as a tanner would use to make leather. The difference in making parchment was the next step: the skin was soaked in water, stretched tightly in a frame, and then repeatedly shaved with a broad round knife called a lunette. The skin was allowed to dry slowly under tension. This sustained stretching and scraping reshaped the fibres of the skin and encouraged them to lie parallel, thus producing a smooth flexible writing surface.

Because each piece of parchment was made by a time-consuming and skilled process from a whole animal skin, parchment was an expensive resource. It has been estimated by specialists in medieval animal husbandry that a herd of about five hundred cattle could produce about seventy calf-skins each year, and some of these might have been needed to make leather. St Margaret's Gospel-book is small: each page is now roughly seventeen and a half centimetres high and eleven wide, but it has been trimmed at some point in its history and the pages would originally have been a bit larger.

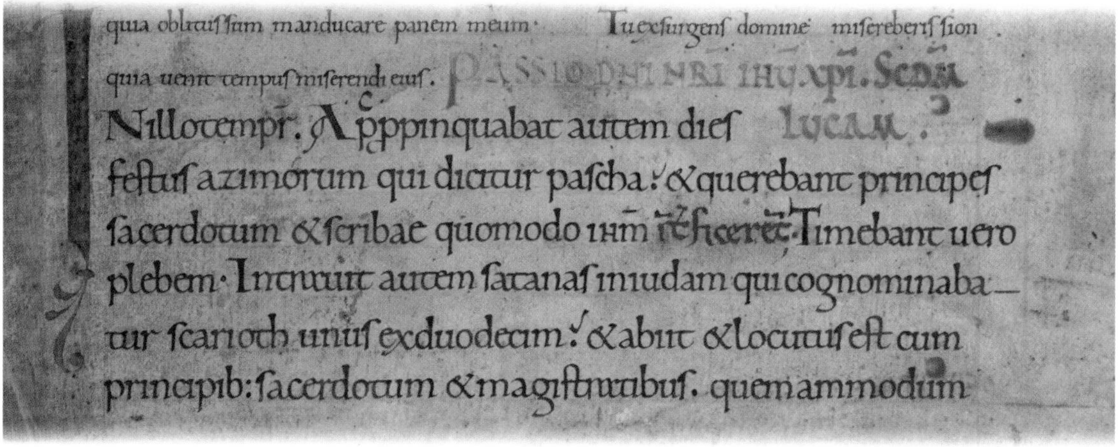

quia obliatus sum manducare panem meum · Tu exsurgens domine misereberis sion
quia uenit tempus miserendi eius. PASSIO DNI NRI IHU XPI. Scdm
Nillo tempr. Appinquabat autem dies LUCAM.
festus azimorum qui dicitur pascha · & querebant principes
sacerdotum & scribae quomodo ihm ficeret. Timebant uero
plebem · Intrauit autem satanas in iudam qui cognominaba
tur scarioth unius exduodecim · & abiit & locutus est cum
principib: sacerdotum & magistratibus. quemammodum

FIGURE 15

The piece of script shown here was written by Eadwig 'the Fat', a Canterbury scribe who made luxurious manuscripts for the gift market in the 1010s and 1020s. His script is highly calligraphic, and he was probably also the illuminator for some of the manuscripts he wrote.

In the first half of the eleventh century Ælfric Bata, a monastic teacher at Christ Church Canterbury, wrote some dialogues to help his pupils learn to speak Latin. In this section one of the masters says that the scribes of the monastery write many books and earn lots of money for themselves, and then a man asks someone to write or sell him a book:[9]

Customer: How many coins must I give you for one missal?

Boy: If you want it you must give me two pounds of silver [worth 480 pence]. And if you don't want it, someone else will. This is a valuable thing, and someone else should buy it more dearly than you.

Customer: Even if someone else wants to be so foolish, I don't. I want to be cautious and buy it for the right price, for a price my friends will say it's worth, that is a fair price.

Boy: But how much will you give me?

Customer: I don't want to pay quite that much.

Boy: But what do you want then, how many coins will you pay, or how many mancuses?

Customer: Believe me, I don't dare give you more or buy it more dearly. Take this, if you want, it's not worth more; I'll pay

you twelve mancuses [worth 360 pence] and count them out into your hand. What else can I do? I'll do nothing other than what you want.

Boy: Count the coins out now so I can tell if they're valuable and whether they're pure silver.

Customer: I will do. [In the classroom the boys could practice counting to twelve in Latin.]

Boy: Certainly these are all good ones!

Customer: Indeed they are.

Prices for land in Anglo-Saxon charters vary greatly, but for this much money the customer could certainly have bought himself a smallish estate, sufficient to support several families.

Oxford, Bodleian Library, MS. Lat. liturg. d. 3, 4r

When first made it contained forty leaves (two were cut out at some stage, probably because they were blank and could be reused for another purpose). It would therefore only have taken three or four skins to make the entire book. Today it would cost in the region of three hundred pounds to buy this much parchment.

Design

The prepared parchment was passed on to the scribe (though the scribe might have been the same person who had prepared the parchment). The scribe, of course, had to be a literate individual, and if not a monk or a nun, at this period they had probably been taught in a monastic school. The scribe might even still have been at school, since writing without artificial light took a toll on the eyes and was probably largely a young person's business. Because it is quite likely that the book was made at a nunnery where Margaret probably spent her youth, I shall refer to the scribe as 'she', though it is possible that the book was made by a man.

A medieval scriptorium in the sense of a large room where lots of scribes worked together, as depicted in Umberto Eco's novel *The Name of the Rose*, did not really exist at this time in England. A monastic scribe would normally have worked in the cloisters, sheltered by a roof and a wall on one side, but otherwise exposed to the elements. They got more natural light this way, but there are stories of how work on manuscripts had to be stopped over the winter because the scribes could not write in the cold. At this stage monasteries also did not have a library in the sense of a dedicated room: books used in services, like missals and psalters, would be kept in the church, while books for study, like copies of Augustine's *Confessions* and Bede's *Ecclesiastical History*, were kept in bookcases or chests in the cloister, perhaps set in alcoves in the wall. They were probably also read in the cloister. Books with very valuable decorated covers might be kept in the treasury.

Set up in the cloister the scribe needed a sloping, rather than flat, writing desk, and a place to put an inkpot and the text she was going to copy. The dry parchment was 'pounced' to remove any remaining grease; this involved rubbing it with pounce, a powder made from ground pumice and cuttlefish bone. But before the scribe of St Margaret's Gospel-book could start writing, she had to consider the size and layout of the book. It is possible to make a small book by taking a pile of sheets of paper or parchment, folding it in half, and sewing or stapling through the fold; modern notebooks and magazines are often made this way. But you cannot make a thick book like this because the fold becomes cumbersome and unmanageable. In the Middle

According to Pliny the Elder, parchment was invented by King Eumenes II of Pergamum in the second century BC when an Egyptian embargo on the export of papyrus forced the invention of a new writing surface.[10] (The Egyptians were worried that the library at Pergamum might grow to rival that of Alexandria.) Parchment is far tougher than paper or papyrus, especially in damp climates, and survives very well down the centuries — British Acts of Parliament are still recorded on parchment for this reason. Used parchment could be scraped down and washed for reuse, a process known as palimpsesting. Some texts only survive because the original words can still be read under the added script.

SĊS LY CAS
EUAH GEL.

Ages, books were made of a series of small booklets bound together, much like modern hardbacks.

The scribe had to consider how much space she would need in the book, and she needed to assemble loosely each booklet, or 'quire', before she started writing in it. To make the first booklet of the St Margaret's Gospel-book the scribe took four sheets of parchment, each sheet probably about eighteen centimetres high by twenty-four wide, roughly three quarters of A4 size. She placed them in a pile, taking care that the bottom sheet had the hair side, the outer side when the skin was on the animal, facing downwards. The second lowest sheet had flesh side facing downwards; the third, hair side facing downwards; and the top sheet had flesh side facing downwards. She then folded the sheets together in half down the middle, to make a booklet of eight leaves or 'folios', containing sixteen pages in total. This attention to the way the hair and flesh sides of the sheets were arranged before folding meant that in every opening of the booklet both the right-hand and left-hand pages were the same side of the parchment, either flesh facing flesh or hair facing hair. This was good practice because the hair side of the parchment was naturally a little darker and rougher than the flesh side, and sometimes still showed pores. If hair faced flesh in an opening then the contrast between the surfaces would detract from the appearance of the book. (In the earliest period of book-production in Ireland and England parchment was so thoroughly prepared before writing that an almost suede-like texture was produced on both sides, making hair and flesh pretty much indistinguishable: they therefore followed a different practice in arranging the sheets in the quire. Scholars still argue about which are the hair and flesh sides of the parchment in the Book of Kells, for example.)

The scribe of St Margaret's Gospel-book took an extra care over the construction of her book; she worked out where the decorated pages would be and made sure that these leaves were made of stiffer, very well-prepared parchment, which gave a better surface to take illumination. This was very easy to do for the first quire, because the St Matthew decoration would naturally be placed in the first opening of the book; but the other decorated pages fall in the middle of quires, so must have taken more thought to arrange. In total St Margaret's Gospel-book comprised five quires, the first four of eight leaves and the last of only six. (A further two folios were added later at the start.)

Once the scribe had a quire assembled she needed to design the page and make rulings for the writing to follow. Each page needed vertical lines to bound each side of the writing area, and horizontal lines for the writing to rest on. To rule the page she opened the sheets out flat again, and used a knife or sharp point to make prick marks; these were placed at the top and bottom of each sheet to guide the vertical lines, and at regular intervals down each side to guide the horizontal lines. She then used a hard point, probably

FIGURE 16
As is usual with evangelist portraits, Luke is here portrayed as a writer, in this case with a scroll rather than a book. Luke is holding his quill in his left hand, with the tip turned towards him, and he seems to be scrutinizing the cut of the nib; this becomes clearer when compared with another picture of St Mark, from Cambridge, Pembroke College, MS. 302, Fig. 17. Presumably this image is adapted from a picture of an evangelist checking the cut of his quill, a common theme in Gospel-books of this era, but the artist has replaced the knife which should be in his right hand with the scroll which indicates that he is an author.
Oxford, Bodleian Library, MS. Lat. liturg. f. 5, 21v

FIGURE 17

Boethius drafts his famous
Consolation of Philosophy on a pair
of wax tablets. A wax tablet like
this was made of two flat pieces
of wood, each coated with a thin
layer of wax surrounded by a
raised edge. These two tablets
could be hinged together down
the side with thongs, so that the
diptych could be closed to
protect the surface and carried
around like a notebook.
Sometimes several wax tablets,
the inner ones double-sided, were
hinged together to form a small
booklet. The scribe wrote on the
wax by scratching with a pointed
stylus. The advantage of writing
on wax tablets was that it was less
expensive than parchment, and
the wax could be smoothed flat
and reused; the stylus would
usually have one sharp end for
writing, and one flat end for
smoothing out the wax.
Oxford, Bodleian Library, MS. Auct. F. 6.
5, vii verso

a metal stylus, and a flat edge to rule the lines between these prickmarks. The
advantage of using a hard point to inscribe the ruling was that the resulting
groove was visible on both sides of the page — in fact several sheets or even a
whole quire could be ruled in one go — and the rulings were not intrusive when
the book was finished. At this period pencil or lead plummet was very rarely
used for ruling in England, but it became more popular and eventually took over
as the preferred method, and in the later Middle Ages coloured ink was often
used, making the ruled frame for the script a decorative feature of the page.

WRITING

The word ink comes ultimately from a Greek word meaning to burn, because
it bites into the page (unlike paint, which is absorbed but does not react with
the surface). There were various recipes for ink in the Middle Ages, and it is
noticeable that Insular and Anglo-Saxon scribes wrote with much blacker ink
than their continental contemporaries, who used mid-brown ink. One
common way to make ink required a particular type of oak gall, the hard
round balls like brown marbles which are formed on oak twigs when a gall
wasp lays its eggs in the bud. A solution made from these was mixed with
gum arabic and soot to make ink; St Margaret's Gospel-book is written in
very dark ink, which probably had a lot of soot in it.

St Margaret's Gospel-book also contains gold ink which the scribe used
to write the beginning of each Gospel as well as headings and initial letters.
This was made by suspending powdered gold in a gum arabic solution; it
could then be used with a quill pen like normal ink, in a technique known as
'chrysography'.

To write on parchment a scribe used a quill pen made from one of the
first five flight feathers of a goose; the word 'pen' comes from the Latin *penna*,
feather. Feathers of other birds like peacocks, owls, and swans could also be
used: a crow's feather, for example, produced a particularly fine pen which
could be used for tiny script or for intricate decoration. The fine fronds of
the feather were stripped from the barrel of the quill, leaving a hollow tube
of material similar in flexibility and strength to a human fingernail. (Some
pictures of scribes show a few tufts of feather fronds left at the very end of
the quill, but certainly most of them were removed.) The stripped quill was
then cut at the end to produce a shape like the nib of a modern fountain
pen, with a slit down the middle of the nib to hold ink. The shape of the
quill can be clearly seen in the Luke image in Margaret's Gospel-book (see
Fig. 16). Modern professional calligraphers often still prefer to write with a
quill on parchment, which gives a very different feeling from writing with a
metal nib on paper: the parchment takes the ink very smoothly, reducing the
blotchiness often seen when using dip-pens on paper, and the quill's
flexibility allows more fluent movement.

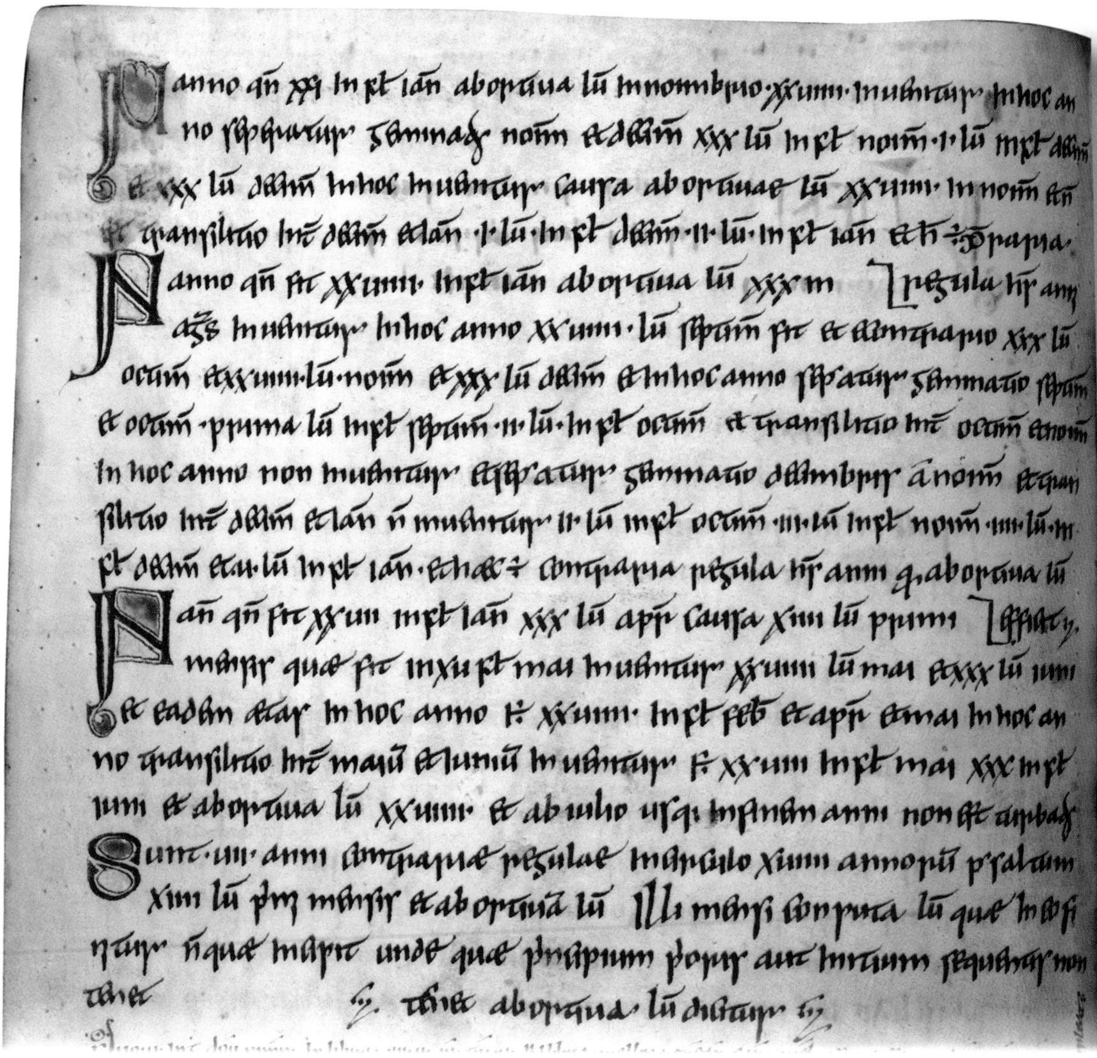

FIGURE 19

Insular minuscule is descended
from Roman scripts. It developed
in Christian Ireland in the period
after the fall of Rome at a time
when it was both a flourishing
centre of scholarly activity and
relatively isolated from the rest of
the world. It can be the most
beautiful of scripts when well-
written, but some letterforms are
strange to modern eyes; for
example, 'r' can look like a
modern 'n', and 's' like a modern
'r' with a tail. Insular script was
used for Latin in England until it
was replaced by Caroline
minuscule, after which it was
used only for texts in English.
Oxford, Bodleian Library, MS. Auct. F. 4.
32, 22v

FIGURE 20

We can tell that St Margaret's Gospel-book was written in England in the second or third quarters of the eleventh century from the type of Caroline minuscule used by the scribe. It is large and round in appearance, and has letterforms typical of English script at this period. During the Renaissance scholars rejected the spiky obscurity of Gothic script and revived Caroline minuscule, which they had seen in Carolingian manuscripts of the Classical texts they studied. They called it *littera antiqua*. Their script was then copied to make fonts for printed books, and because of this modern fonts are still often based on Caroline minuscule. You can see this particularly in the printed forms of 'a' and 'g', which are like those used in Caroline minuscule, and are shaped differently from how most people would write them by hand.

Oxford, Bodleian Library, MS. Lat. liturg. f. 5, 32v

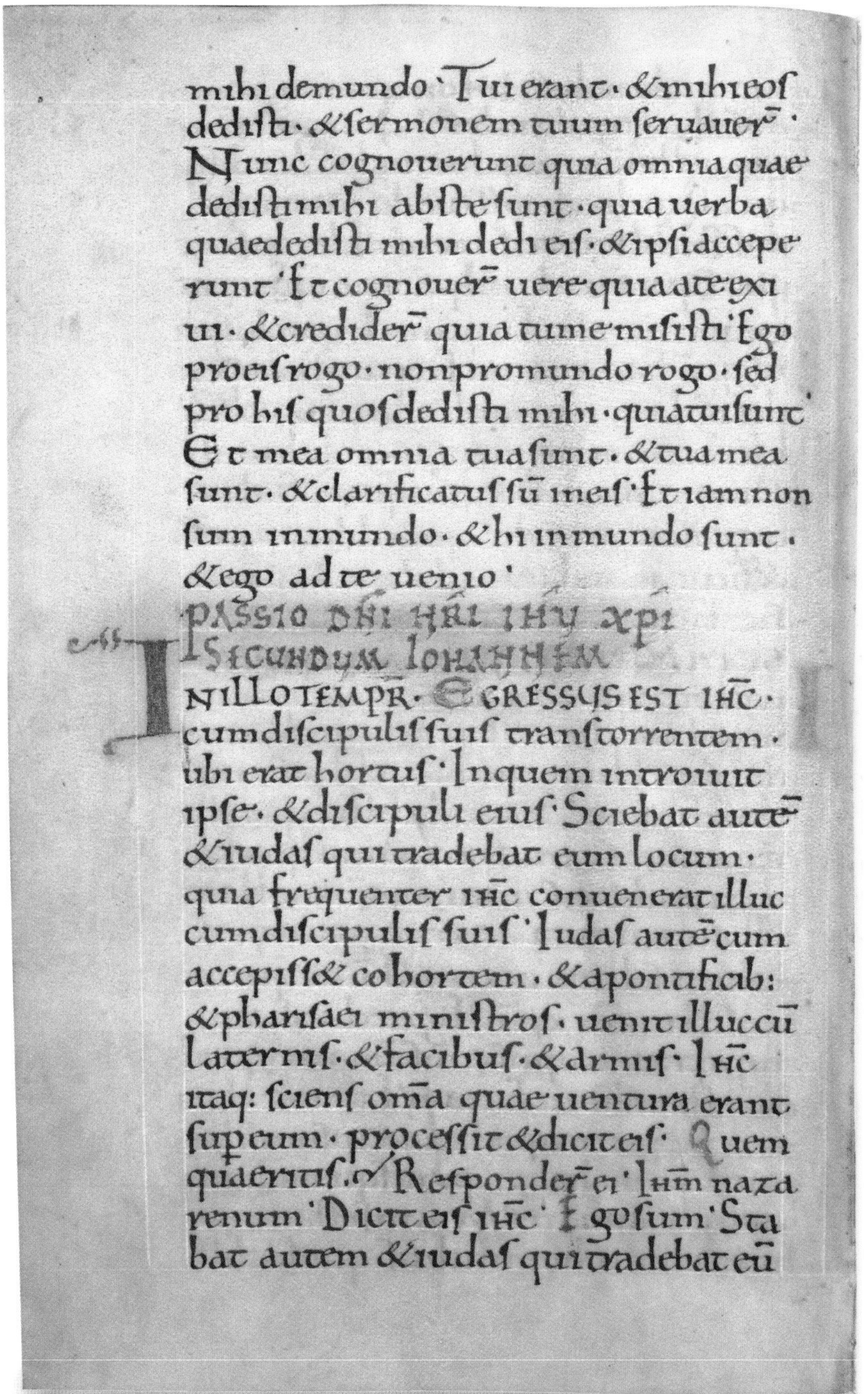
mihi demundo · Tui erant · & mihi eos
dedisti · & sermonem tuum seruauer̄ ·
Nunc cognouerunt quia omnia quae
dedisti mihi abs te sunt · quia uerba
quae dedisti mihi dedi eis · & ipsi accepe
runt · Et cognouer̄ uere quia a te exi
ui · & crediderunt quia tu me misisti · Ego
pro eis rogo · non pro mundo rogo · sed
pro his quos dedisti mihi · quia tui sunt ·
Et mea omnia tua sunt · & tua mea
sunt · & clarificatus sū in eis · Et iam non
sum in mundo · & hi in mundo sunt ·
& ego ad te uenio ·
PASSIO DNI NRI IHU XPI
SECUNDUM IOHANNEM
IN ILLO TEMPR · EGRESSUS EST IHC ·
cum discipulis suis trans torrentem ·
ubi erat hortus · In quem introiuit
ipse · & discipuli eius · Sciebat autē
& iudas qui tradebat eum locum ·
quia frequenter ihc conuenerat illuc
cum discipulis suis · Iudas autē cum
accepisset cohortem · & a pontificib:
& pharisaei ministros · uenit illuc cū
laternis · & facibus · & armis · Ihc
itaq: sciens omā quae uentura erant
sup eum · processit & dicit eis · Quem
quaeritis · Responder̄ ei · Ihm naza
renum · Dicit eis ihc · Ego sum · Sta
bat autem & iudas qui tradebat eū

BEATVS

VIR QVI NON
ABIIT IN CONSILIO
IMPIORVM ET IN UIA PECCA
TORVM NON STETIT ET IN
CATHEDRA PESTILENTIAE
NON SEDIT:

The scribe would, of course, need to know what she was going to write.
St Margaret's Gospel-book consists of a series of extracts from the Gospels,
so it would have been easy for the scribe to find an exemplar to copy, but
when writing a more complex work or composing a new text the scribe
would probably draft it first on wax tablets.

Once the quire was assembled and ruled, the ink mixed, the quill
sharpened, and the texts chosen, the scribe could start to write. In her left
hand she would hold a knife, which had three important uses: it held the
page flat while writing; it could scrape out any mistakes she made; and she
could use it to resharpen the quill as it got blunted by use.

Because all medieval books had to be written out by hand, clarity and
uniformity in writing were very important and handwriting was not the
expression of individuality that it is now. Certainly not everyone could write,
and writing was taught as a craft. We can see fashions and styles of writing
arising and disappearing over time and in different places, in the same way
that we might nowadays recognize generically French handwriting from its
distinctive way of writing the numbers 1 and 7. Because of this, script can be
very useful for working out roughly when and where a manuscript was
written. Manuscripts from England at this period were never explicitly dated
and are rarely securely datable from their text, so the study of script, known
as 'palaeography', can be of vital importance in dating and localising
manuscripts.

The scribe of St Margaret's Gospel-book wrote a variety of a script
called Caroline minuscule. This script gets its name from its assocation with
the court of King Charlemagne (768–814). It is a very clear and legible way
of writing, and was eventually used across most of Western Europe. England
was relatively late in adopting it, but in the middle of the tenth century it
was introduced by ecclesiastical reformers. It became the standard type of
script for writing Latin in England, although texts in Old English continued
to be written in Insular minuscule.

A specifically English style of Caroline minuscule was developed in the
eleventh century, and this is how we know that St Margaret's Gospel-book
was written in England. English Caroline minuscule can be recognized by its
round 'aspect' or appearance on the page, its density, and the thick pen that
was used, as well as by specific letter-forms such as 'a', 'g', 'r', and 's'.
Although the scribe of St Margaret's Gospel-book writes clearly and legibly,
her script is not hugely calligraphic, and occasionally it looks a little clumsy.
From the script we can estimate that the manuscript was written sometime
in the middle of the eleventh century; on palaeographical grounds it would
be unwise to try to be more specific than to the second or third quarters of
the eleventh century.

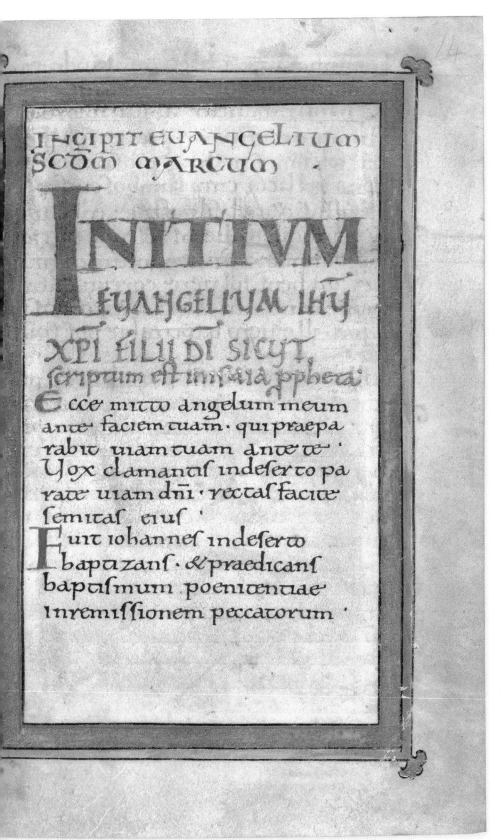

INCIPIT EUANGELIUM
SCDM MARCUM

INITIVM

EUANGELIVM IHV

XPI FILII DI SICVT
scriptum est inisaia ppheta·
Ecce mitto angelum meum
ante faciem tuam· qui praepa
rabit uiam tuam ante te·
Uox clamantis indeserto pa
rate uiam dni· rectas facite
semitas eius·
Fuit iohannes indeserto
baptizans· &praedicans
baptismum poenitentiae
inremissionem peccatorum·

FIGURE 22

The opening of the Gospel of St Mark, the evangelist portrait facing the first words of the text. The title 'The start of the Gospel according to Mark' is written in a type of round script called Uncial, and the first word of the Gospel, *initium*, is in large Square capitals of the type that the Romans used on monuments. The next few lines are Rustic capitals, a narrow capital script, and the end of the first verse is written in plain minuscule, or lowercase, script, but still in gold. Then the text continues in normal black ink. This way of working through a series of types of script in decreasing order of grandness at the start of a text is an old Insular practice.

Oxford, Bodleian Library, MS. Lat. liturg. f. 5, 13v–14r

FIGURE 23 *left*

St Matthew in Margaret's Gospel-book; he sits writing his Gospel, framed by two curtains. His stool is set on the earth, signified by the curvy lines made with different intensities of the same shade of brown. His feet, however, rest not on the ground but on a footstool, emphasising his holy status. The drape of Matthew's clothes is fluidly modelled to show the shape of his limbs beneath. Like all the evangelists in Margaret's Gospel-book he wears a tunic under an over-robe in a contrasting colour, and his book is picked out in gold to symbolize its importance.

Oxford, Bodleian Library, MS. Lat. liturg. f. 5, 3v

FIGURE 24 *right*

St Luke in the Hereford Gospels, a mid-eleventh-century book of Gospel extracts. He sits with his pen tucked behind his ear, preparing to do something to his book with a knife — perhaps he is about to rule lines for the text. The palette of colours is very like that in St Margaret's Gospel-book, but more intense. This manuscript was made in the mid-eleventh century, probably for private use, but was at Hereford or Worcester by the end of the eleventh century.

Cambridge, Pembroke College, MS. 302, 60v

SCS IOHANNES
EVANGELISTA

ILLUMINATION

Any illumination in a manuscript was usually added after it was written, in blank spaces purposely left by the scribe. Margaret's Gospel-book contains four pictures, one of each evangelist, which was the usual scheme of decoration for a complete copy of the Gospels. Although Margaret's manuscript contains only extracts from the Gospels and not the whole text, these extracts are arranged in the order they would be found in a full Gospel-book, and the beginning of each Gospel is included; this made it possible for the same decorative scheme to be followed. The evangelist portrait is on the verso, or left-hand side, of the opening, and faces the first words of the Gospel written in golden script.

In the later Middle Ages high-grade book-production was usually split up into a number of different jobs each done by a separate specialist: a scribe would write the text, a rubricator would add coloured chapter headings, an initialler would draw the decorated initials, and another artist would paint the miniatures. But when St Margaret's Gospel-book was made this sort of specialisation had not yet developed, and it may be that the scribe also painted the pictures — although the illumination seems rather more accomplished than the script.

The pictures were drawn in ink, probably over drafted lines scratched out with a hard point, then coloured with washes of paint. The artist used the same pigment in different strengths to create intensity of tone. She used just four main colours; blue, green, yellow, and orange-brown. Since non-destructive techniques for analysing manuscript pigments are still in their infancy, we cannot be sure exactly how the artist achieved her colours, though we can take an educated guess from what we know to have happened in other manuscripts and from later medieval recipes. The blue was probably made from a plant extract, perhaps imported indigo but more probably native woad. It was mixed with gum arabic or with glair (beaten and strained eggwhite) so that it would bind to the parchment. The green would have been prepared from verdigris, the green rust which occurs naturally on copper and brass, or which can be provoked with vinegar or by burying the metal in a dungheap. The yellow could have been made with orpiment, a sulphide of arsenic found around hotsprings and volcanic sites, but this is highly poisonous and reacts badly with verdigris and red lead. More probably an organic plant-based dye was used; *genista tinctoria*, the dyer's broom, provides a good strong yellow. The orange-brown could have been made from the usual sources of red: toasted lead, minium (from which the word 'miniature' to describe manuscript illuminations derives); or vermilion, made from cinnabar, a toxic ore of mercury. But there would have been less poisonous possibilities here too: ochre, umber and sienna are all types of brown pigment made from mined earth, and a reddish-brown tint could

FIGURE 25

St John is the only evangelist in St Margaret's Gospel-book shown without a bookrest: instead he has the book on his lap. His fingers are arranged for writing but he has no quill. This may have been an oversight on the artist's part, or perhaps she has adapted her source to show John blessing rather than writing his book. John had a slightly higher status than the other evangelists as the disciple whom Jesus loved and to whom he entrusted his mother from the cross, and also because he was the recipient of the Revelation of the Apocalypse which forms the last book of the Bible. In St Margaret's Gospel-book he is the only evangelist shown with both architectural decoration and a curtain, and his throne, which has a back, is much grander than the stools on which the others sit.

Oxford, Bodleian Library, MS. Lat. liturg. f. 5, 30v

FIGURE 26 *left*
St Matthew the Evangelist in an eleventh-century Gospel-book probably from Peterborough or Bury St Edmunds. He looks up at his symbol, the winged man or angel, who is bringing text from above. This book is much larger in size than Margaret's Gospel-book and consequently it is possible for the composition to be more complex; but the main elements, the figure on a stool with a pen and book, between two tucked-up curtains, are the same.

Cambridge, Pembroke College, MS. 301, 10v

easily have been obtained from the iron-rich clay found (for example) in the West Country of England; or the roots of the various species of madder plant also produce a red dye. As well as these pigments the artist used white paint, made simply from chalk, to pick out highlights.

The pictures also have golden areas. These were not produced by applying sheets of gold leaf, which is the most common method of gilding medieval manuscripts; instead they were painted using gold ink, like the decorated opening words on the page facing each evangelist. Gold ink is a more expensive but less complex way of applying gold to a picture. It often results in the 'reddish-gold' hue noticed by Turgot in his description of the manuscript.

Almost all surviving Anglo-Saxon Gospel-books have the same basic pattern of decoration, and the illuminator of St Margaret's Gospel-book

FIGURE 27 *right*
Architectural decoration above an arch, and tucked-up curtains, as found in St Margaret's Gospel-book, are both common motifs in late Anglo-Saxon author-portraits. This very fluid line drawing of St Jerome shows both. This picture was added to a late tenth-century manuscript of Jerome's *Life of St Paul the First Hermit* at Canterbury *circa* 1070. Jerome wears the tonsure of a monk and the Holy Spirit, in the form of a dove, whispers inspiration in his ear.

Cambridge, Corpus Christi College, MS. 389, 1v

will have taken it for granted that each Gospel would be preceded by an evangelist portrait. The evangelists are shown as authors, seated in an architectural setting, writing their Gospels; the pattern derives from author-portraits of late antiquity. However, she will have had some opportunity within those bounds to choose how exactly to portray them, and she probably planned out her compositions on a wax tablet or scraps of parchment. The small size of the manuscript demands a straightforward composition, and she has put the pictures inside plain frames. Late Anglo-Saxon manuscript art often included complex floriate borders with rosettes at the corners, like the borders in the 'Missal' of Robert of Jumièges (see Fig. 28); the artist of St Margaret's Gospel-book does not use these, perhaps because they are complex to construct, or perhaps because there was insufficient space for them. She has also not included the symbols with which the evangelists were often pictured. These come from visions of God in Ezekiel and Revelation; the angel, lion, calf, and eagle were held to represent Matthew, Mark, Luke, and John respectively. Sometimes the evangelists were even pictured with the heads of their symbol; for example John would be shown as a man with an eagle's head.

Matthew, Mark and John have architectural seats while Luke sits on a lion-clawed stool, and is also the only one carrying a scroll rather than a book. The artist probably practiced and planned out her designs on a wax tablet or on scraps of spare parchment.

In style the pictures of St Margaret's Gospel-book, like the script, are distinctively English, and find their closest parallels in other manuscripts from the middle of the eleventh century. Some of them have been illustrated elsewhere in this book; the Hereford Gospels (see Figs. 17 and 23), the Pembroke 301 Gospels (see Fig. 26), and the Judith Gospels (see Fig. 50). The 'Missal' of Robert of Jumièges (see Fig. 29), made in the early eleventh century, shows a technique of using a wash of curvy painted lines to represent landscape, similar to that found in St Margaret's Gospel-book.

The Crowland Psalter, made after 1057 (probably in the early 1060s) at Crowland, provides a close parallel to the style of St Margaret's Gospel-book. The picture of Christ trampling the beasts (see Fig. 30), shows a tall elongated figure like those of St Margaret's evangelists. The tones of the pigments and the line drawing and wash method of painting are also similar to those in St Margaret's Gospel-book.

BINDING

There were two aspects to the binding of a medieval manuscript; the practical and the decorative. The aims of the practical side of the operation were to fasten the booklets, or quires, together in sequence in such a way that the book was flexible and easily opened, and to attach hard boards to the manuscript to serve as protective front and back covers.

FIGURE 28
This Flemish evangelist picture, from the middle of the eleventh century, shows what a different effect can be produced by the same image in another style. St Mark is here shown within a plain gold frame, seated before his open book, and trimming his quill. However, the picture is entirely painted, with no part of the parchment left blank. Stronger colours have been used, and the artist has filled in geometrical patterns in the background. The style is stiffer, and the treatment of the drapery in particular is less fluid. The evangelist symbol, a winged lion, is shown bringing the first words of the Gospel down from the top right-hand corner, where concentric wavy circular lines represent the divine. The picture was added to an earlier Breton Gospel-book on the orders of Bishop Leofric of Exeter, either circa 1040 when he was in Lotharingia, or by a Flemish artist whom he commissioned specially after 1046 when he was based in Devon.
Oxford, Bodleian Library, MS. Auct. D. 2. 16, 72v

FIGURE 29

This is the earliest surviving picture of the deposition, the removal of the dead Christ from the cross, in English art, from the 'Missal' of Robert of Jumièges.

As well as the use of washes of pigment, this image shows the complex foliate borders, known as the 'Winchester style', which are often found in manuscript

illumination from the last century of Anglo-Saxon England.

Rouen, Bibliothèque municipale, MS. Y.6 (274), 72r

Binding took place after writing; unless a short text was added to blank pages in an older book, scribes wrote on loose unbound sheets. The binding might have been done by the scribe, or by another craftsman. Often the scribe would leave clues in the manuscript to help the binder get the quires in the right order, perhaps numbering the quires 'i', 'ii', etc., or perhaps writing the first word of the next quire on the back page of each quire, but there are no such clues in St Margaret's Gospel-book.

Once the binder had the quires in a pile in the correct order she would take a sharp needle, some strong thread, and several leather thongs each with a short slit in it. These slit thongs were to go across the spine of the binding, at right angles to the closed quires; on old books you often see a series of ridges across the thickness of the spine, formed by the thongs or bands under the leather covering. St Margaret's Gospel-book was sewn onto four split thongs.

The binder pierced the first quire through the centre fold and then sewed the thread around both sides of the split part of the thong. Each place where the thread pierced the quire was called a sewing station, and had its own thong. The binder then took the thread along to the next sewing station, pushed it through the centre of the quire, and sewed it to the next split thong. Once she had sewn all four sewing stations of the first quire to their own thong she then did the same to the remaining four quires, sewing them onto the thongs close to the preceding quires. When she had done this the inside of the book was assembled, the quires sewn onto the flexible leather thongs. The ends of the thongs could now be attached to the back and front boards. These covers were usually made of wood, often oak, and were thick enough that holes could be drilled within their thickness. The leather thongs of the binding were fed into these holes or grooves, and the thongs were then pegged into place. If the scribe had deliberately left the first and last folios of the book blank then these could be stuck down with animal glue or paste onto the boards, to attach the book more firmly to the wooden covers. It looks as though the scribe of St Margaret's Gospel-book had not left a blank folio at the front but had left a spare folio at the back. This last folio was pasted down to the back board, and an extra pair of folios were sewn into the front of the manuscript so that the first folio of this could be pasted to the front board. A strip of parchment might also be pasted down the spine of a manuscript to strengthen it, but probably this was not necessary for books as thin as St Margaret's Gospel-book.

The outside of the whole structure, both boards and spine, could now be covered with leather. (Sometimes this was done before the pastedown was attached.) Especially precious books might have a 'chemise', a further cover made of soft leather or material. Although attached to the binding this would be larger than it so that when the book was closed it could be completely wrapped around it, and so that when the book was open it automatically formed a cloth for it to lie on.

Many medieval bindings also incorporated clasps to keep the book shut.
Because parchment is an organic material, from the round surface of an
animal's back, it cockles unless kept compressed flat. Medieval manuscripts
were kept in chests, not pressed together on shelves as is usual for modern
books, so clasps served a useful purpose. The poem about the river episode
states that St Margaret's Gospel-book was on this occasion carried
'uncovered and unfastened', which suggests that the original binding had
clasps, but probably no attached chemise. (It may have had its own book
satchel, an old Gaelic custom.)

We also know both from the poem and from Turgot's description that
the manuscript had at least one cloth to protect the decoration. These would
have been kept between the decorated pages at the start of each Gospel, so
that the pigments and gold did not either get damaged or rub off on the
facing page. Similar protective veils sometimes still survive in later
manuscripts, usually sewn onto the page, though this presumably cannot
have been the case in St Margaret's Gospel-book because no sewing
holes survive.

The original binding has long gone from this manuscript, and the
pastedowns had been lifted from the boards and turned instead into flyleaves
by the late sixteenth century when John Stow wrote his name on the back of
the last folio. Binding structures are very vulnerable to loss because the whole
point of a binding is to absorb the wear that would otherwise affect the more
fragile manuscript. The current binding was made when the manuscript
underwent conservation work at the Bodleian Library in 1993, and the
previous seventeenth-century binding is now kept separately.

FIGURE 31 *left* It was usual to have pastedowns, and
perhaps some protective flyleaves, in a manuscript
even if there were no suitable blank folios. Scrap
parchment was employed for this purpose, mostly
taken from old books which had outlived their
usefulness. Many Anglo-Saxon manuscripts only
survive as fragments used as pastedowns, fly leaves,
or spine-strengthening strips in later manuscripts. If
a scrap pastedown was eventually removed from a
manuscript, perhaps when it was rebound, the biting
nature of ink meant that it might leave an offset of
its text behind on the wood. This picture shows the
sole ghostly remnant of a grand Anglo-Saxon missal
from Bury St Edmunds, an offset on the back board
of a thirteenth-century manuscript.
Oxford, Bodleian Library, MS. Bodley 356, back board

FIGURE 33

St Margaret's Gospel-book had a
'treasure binding', covered all over
in gold and jewels. We know from
other literary sources that many
medieval Gospel-books were given
richly-decorated bindings, but gold,
jewels, and beautifully-carved ivory
were vulnerable to being stolen or
reused. Only a few medieval
treasure bindings still survive. This
example is from a book of Gospel
extracts written in England for
Judith of Flanders, wife of Tostig,
earl of Northumbria (*See Family
Tree, p.106*). Tostig was Earl
Harold's brother and the brother-
in-law of Edward the Confessor, as
well as the sworn oath-brother of
Malcolm. After Tostig's death in
1066 his sons went to Scandinavia,
but Judith returned to her family in
Flanders, and in around 1070 was
married off to Welf IV, count of
Bavaria. She took her books with
her, and left them to the church at
Weingarten; this jewelled binding is
probably English in origin, but
could perhaps have been added to
the manuscript in Flanders. This
binding shows Christ in a
mandorla, holding a book and
making a gesture of blessing. In the
corners are the four signs of the
evangelists. The borders are set
with jewels, and the metal is
decorated in a filigree style. The
binding of Margaret's Gospel-book
is likely to have looked similar,
although probably it would have
been simpler in design, as Judith's
book is somewhat larger.

New York, Pierpont Morgan, MS. M.709,
front board

The lost treasure binding

If Margaret could see it now probably she would not immediately recognize
her favourite book, because it has lost one of its most striking and important
features: the decorated binding. Turgot describes the manuscript as 'covered
all over with jewels and gold', which shows that in Margaret's time it had a
decorated metal 'treasure binding' over its wooden boards. This sort of
binding was vulnerable because of its obvious value and portable nature, and
very few medieval examples survive. We do not know when Margaret's
Gospel-book lost its treasure binding, but it is very unlikely that it survived
the Middle Ages. It had gone by the time the book was rebound for Lord
William Howard in the early seventeenth century.

Surviving treasure bindings show us what Margaret's book now lacks.
People's first impression of the manuscript then would have been very
different; the painting and the gold inside the book, which attract us today,
were only the secondary level of decoration. But the decorated binding was
not just there to please the eye; it was a tribute to the importance of the text
inside. Turgot tells us that, although he could not read, Malcolm's respect
and love for his wife led him to kiss and revere her books, on occasion
ordering a goldsmith to embellish a particular one with gold and jewels.

The front and back covers of the lost jewelled binding would have been
made of metal, decorated with gold. It would have had precious stones —
not faceted like modern jewels, but smooth like pebbles — set around the
border of each cover, and in the centre perhaps further stones, or perhaps an
image of some sort like a crucifix.

THE RIVER EPISODE

It is worth remembering that we only know this Gospel-book to have been
Margaret's because of three events: its rescue from the river; the mention of
this as the sole miracle in Turgot's *Life*; and the addition of the poem about
the same event to the front of the manuscript. (Others of Margaret's books
may well survive unidentified.) Without the poem we would not be able to
identify this manuscript as the book Turgot describes — it shows no
signs of ever having been in Scotland. Without Turgot's account of the
miracle, the poem would probably have been held to refer to Edward the
Confessor and Queen Edith, or perhaps William I and Matilda. The two
texts give us information about the book which we cannot gather from the
manuscript itself.

The poem has no need to describe the manuscript it refers to because it
is written inside that same book; but Turgot's *Life* provides some interesting
details about its physical appearance. It is from Turgot that we know the
manuscript had a treasure binding; the poem adds the information that when
the manuscript fell into the river it was carelessly carried, unwrapped, and

FIGURE 32

A surviving thin veil
to protect illumination in a
fifteenth-century German
manuscript. Similar veils were
apparently washed out of St
Margaret's Gospel-book when it fell
in the river. It has sometimes been
questioned whether St Margaret's
Gospel-book ever had veils in it,
since surviving veils are usually sewn
into the manuscript and there are
no sewing marks next to the images
in St Margaret's Gospel-book.
However, this picture shows an
example of a free-standing veil,
which was simply placed into the
manuscript without being secured.
These veils were probably less likely
to survive than sewn-in ones.

Oxford, Bodleian Library, MS. Lat. liturg.
f. 4, 12r

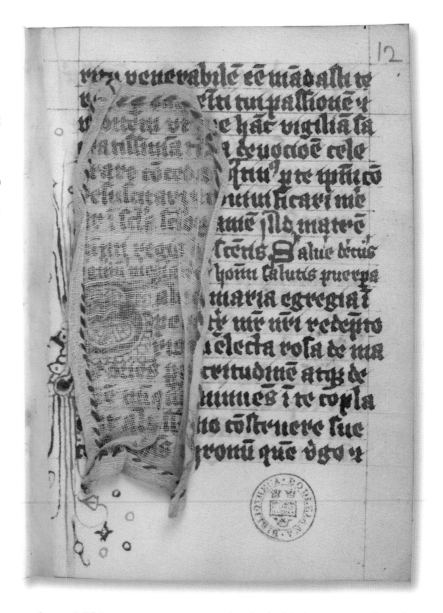

unfastened. If it came to rest open on the riverbed it is easy to see how the
heavy metal boards of the treasure binding would have weighted it down and
prevented its closing, leaving the lighter pages between them exposed to the
currents and very vulnerable. Both the section about the river rescue in
Turgot's *Life* and the poem copied into the front of the manuscript say that
none of the manuscript was damaged except for the endleaves. There are no
signs of water damage in the main part of the volume; and although several
nineteenth- and twentieth-century scholars mentioned that the endleaves
showed such damage, this is not immediately apparent today. The endleaves
are rather battered, but then a certain amount of wear is always to be
expected on these folios, which are naturally more exposed than the main
part of the volume. The cockling of the leaves may have become less

FIGURE 34

The use of manuscripts for swearing oaths was not unusual in the Middle Ages. This illustration is from the Red Book of Darley, a service book which was written in the 1060s at Sherborne in Dorset but which has later provenance in Derbyshire. This manuscript has a sixteenth-century inscription stating that 'this booke was sumtime had in such reverence in Darbieshire that it was comonlie beleved that whosoever should sweare untruelie uppon this booke should run madd'.

Cambridge, Corpus Christi College, MS. 422, p. 53

FIGURE 35

St Margaret's Gospel-book was used for swearing oaths, according to the poem added to its opening pages; the St Augustine Gospels still play a role in modern ceremonial occasions. This book gets its name because it was probably brought to England by St Augustine himself when he was sent by Pope Gregory to convert the English in 597. (If it was not brought by St Augustine then it must have come with one of the subsequent waves of early Italian missionaries to England.) Since the middle of the twentieth century this Gospel-book has been used each time a new archbishop is enthroned at Canterbury. In 1982 when the pope came to Britain for the first time since the Reformation, the Gospel-book was taken to Canterbury Cathedral and placed in the throne there, so that neither the pope nor the archbishop took the most important seat but both gave way to the Gospel.

Cambridge, Corpus Christi College, MS. 286, 125r

pronounced with decades of careful storage and use in the Bodleian: parchment is a flexible substance.

The poem gives the extra information that the Gospel-book was taken by a priest to be used in the swearing of an oath. Oaths were a very important part of medieval life, and played a large part in legal proceedings. Someone could clear themselves of a criminal accusation by getting a certain number of men in good standing to swear an oath supporting them; the number of oath-takers needed depended on the status of the accused and on the alleged crime. (This seems to be the origin of the English system of trial by jury.) In the same way that Bibles are sometimes used to swear in courtroom witnesses in modern times, Gospel-books and relics were often used for the swearing of oaths in the Middle Ages.

The sanctity of the object increased the solemnity of an oath: Harold, last Anglo-Saxon king of England, got himself into trouble because he allegedly swore allegiance to William the Conqueror on some relics which William had cunningly concealed under a cloth. In early medieval times important documents such as grants of land or writs freeing slaves were often copied out into Gospels or other such liturgical books so that the charter gained reflected authority from the manuscript. In these ways religious books could play an important part in legal and political life.

No small amount of time, expense, and craftsmanship went into making Margaret's little Gospel-book. Nonetheless, by the standards of surviving Anglo-Saxon Gospel-books it is quite modest. It is unpretentious in size, text, script, and surviving decoration, and Margaret must have owned more lavish books, at least once she was queen. If we believe Turgot that this was her favourite book even before the miracle of the river then probably it had some sort of personal significance for her. Since the manuscript probably was made in England in the middle of the eleventh century we can hypothesize that she brought it with her when she fled to Scotland, and that it was probably part of her youth at a nunnery, perhaps Wilton. It could have been a gift, though the occasional ineptness of the script might suggest that it was not written by a professional. Perhaps she valued it because it was given to her or made by someone connected with her — or she might even have written it herself at Wilton, where we know young noblewomen like St Edith, King Edgar's daughter, and Queen Edith, Edward the Confessor's wife, engaged in writing. (Although Turgot would presumably have mentioned any such connection if he had known of it.)

Margaret the Holy Queen

THE EARLIEST SOURCES FOR HER LIFE

Several pieces of evidence dating from Margaret's lifetime survive to show that she was widely respected as a virtuous and holy woman from early on.

The Anglo-Saxon Chronicle

The annal for 1067 in the D-manuscript of the *Anglo-Saxon Chronicle*, probably written soon after 1079, shows that in England Margaret was seen as very holy while she was still alive. It tells the story of how Edgar the Ætheling, his mother and sisters, and some nobles, fled to Scotland and were taken in by King Malcolm:

> *Then King Malcolm began to yearn for his [Edgar's] sister Margaret as his wife, but he [Edgar] and all his men refused for a long time, and she herself refused.*[11]

The prose text breaks into verse to describe Margaret's desire to live as a nun:

> *she said that she would have neither him nor anyone*
> *if the High One would allow piety to her*
> *that she in maidenhood might please the mighty Lord*
> *with body and heart in pure restraint in this short life.*

But according to the *Chronicle* God, who sees even the fall of a sparrow, did not allow this because Margaret was able to achieve more good as queen of Scotland:

> *The prescient Creator knew beforehand what he would have done by her, that she would increase God's love in that land and help the king out of the wrong path and direct him and his people to a better way.*

The *Chronicle* quotes St Paul's famous words from I Corinthians 7:14: 'for the unbelieving husband is sanctified by the wife':

FIGURE 36
King Æthelstan presents a book to St Cuthbert in 934. Margaret's connection to the English royal family may account for her devotion to Cuthbert and Durham. Malcolm was present at the laying of the foundation stone of the present Durham Cathedral on 11 August 1093. (It has been suggested that Margaret was there too, but according to Turgot by this point she was rarely able to leave her bed.)
Cambridge, Corpus Christi College, MS. 183, 1r

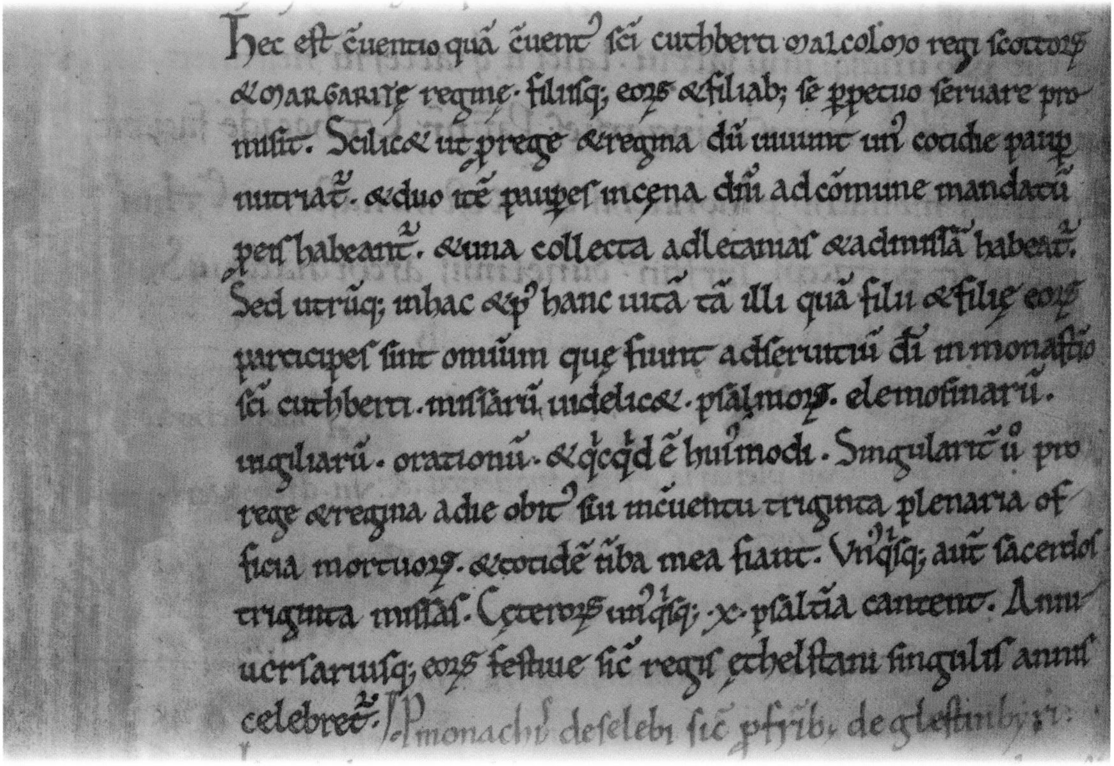

FIGURE 37

The Durham *Liber Vitae* was made in the mid-ninth century at an important Northumbrian church, perhaps at Bede's monastery of Monkwearmouth-Jarrow, but more probably at the bishopric of Lindisfarne. It is a book of commemoration, recording the names of the church's benefactors living and dead, and contains hundreds of names of bishops, kings, hermits, priests, and others, written in alternating gold and silver ink. In 875 the monks of St Cuthbert left Lindisfarne with his relics, forced to move by Viking attacks. In 882 they stopped at Chester-le-Street in County Durham where they settled for just over a century before moving on to Durham itself. In the late eleventh century, perhaps worrying about continuity in the wake of the Norman Conquest, they started to add to their *Liber Vitae* again.

Margaret and Malcolm were written onto the page dedicated to kings, and the names of their eight children were added together to the names in the main body of the book. This page shows Margaret and Malcolm's agreement with the community at Durham, the only one made with a non-ecclesiastical beneficiary.

London, British Library, MS. Cotton Domitian A. VII, 48v

This aforesaid queen afterwards did many useful works in that land for the love of God, and also flourished well in the kingdom as was natural to her. She was sprung of a believing and noble race...

This long excursion in the *Chronicle* shows what a high value was put on Margaret's English ancestry, and that she was already known in England as a holy queen during her lifetime.

The Durham Liber Vitae

Malcolm and Margaret made an agreement with the cathedral at Durham in the 1080s or early 1090s: during their lifetime the monks would feed one poor person for them every day, and two on Maundy Thursday; in their lifetime and after it both they and their children would be in confraternity with the monastery; and at the king and queen's deaths there were to be thirty full offices of the dead, *verba mea* (the penitential psalms) would be said every day, each priest was to sing thirty masses, and the other members of the community would sing ten psalters.[12] The anniversary of their death was to be celebrated every year in the same way as that of King Athelstan: this again shows Margaret being associated with her royal West-Saxon ancestors.

Margaret and Malcolm must have given a substantial donation to the community to have been honoured as such important benefactors. The names of their children were added to the register of the community's friends at the same time.

Correspondence

We know that Margaret wrote to Lanfranc, archbishop of Canterbury 1070–1089, but her letters do not survive. We have one of his replies however, from which it appears that she wrote to him to ask for help in setting up a Benedictine monastery, a daughter-house of Canterbury, at Dunfermline, where she and Malcolm had been married.[13] She has requested that he send a particular brother called Goldwin; this is an Anglo-Saxon name, and presumably she had met him while she was in England. Lanfranc says he is sending her Goldwin and two others to help him.

Although it seems that Margaret and Lanfranc had not met — Lanfranc did not come to England until 1070 — Lanfranc is very affectionate to her. He describes his joy at receiving her letter and his certainty that it was inspired by the Holy Spirit, and begs:

Let there be a mutual exchange between us of prayers and good works.

He touchingly warns her against thinking too highly of him:

I am not what you think I am; but may I be it because you think it.

Lanfranc says that he will be her father and she his daughter, even though he is an unworthy foreigner and she is 'born of a royal race and royally educated'. Lanfranc writes in Latin, and Margaret will have written to him in the same language; she had chaplains who could have helped her with this, but Lanfranc's reference to her being 'royally educated' suggests that she had some Latin literacy, and Turgot's *Life* confirms this.

Another Latin letter addressed to Margaret survives, composed by Theobald of Étampes, 'doctor of Caen'.[14] Theobald, who went on to teach at Oxford and is sometimes credited with being its first lecturer, wrote in a convoluted and impenetrable Latin style, and it is extremely hard to work out what meaning he is trying to convey. It seems that they have had some past correspondence, and that in this letter Theobald asks to return to a position as one of her clerics, even if he should be shipwrecked in the process. He says that her good reputation has spread widely, and that his inability to praise her as she deserves is not to be wondered at: even if all his limbs were to turn into tongues he would not be able to praise her sufficiently.

This letter suggests that Margaret's reputation as a charitable and religious woman who supported clerics had spread overseas. There is one small problem, however; in the letter Theobald addresses Margaret as the daughter of a good king, although Edward the Exile never reigned. Theobald may have thought that Edward the Confessor was her father, or seen him as her adopted father, but it is also possible that he was actually writing to someone else. The only manuscript of this letter was lost, probably in the French Revolution, and we only know it from a seventeenth-century printed book. It is possible that the manuscript said simply 'M.' — medieval manuscripts of letters often have names shortened to just an initial — and that the first editor mistakenly expanded this to Margaret when it should have read Matilda, her daughter and queen of Henry I. Either of these two queens would fit with Theobald's dates.

Goscelin's Life of St Laurence

A Flemish monk called Goscelin came to England in the late 1050s and wrote many Latin works about English saints. These include the *Life and Miracles of St Laurence*, the second archbishop of Canterbury, who died in 619.[15] It includes a story about Queen Margaret visiting his shrine at Laurencekirk in Scotland, to give gifts there 'out of sweet religion'. Goscelin calls her 'beloved of God', exactly the same phrase that Lanfranc used to address her in his surviving letter. However, no woman was ever allowed to enter Laurence's church, and the canons there begged her not to pass the threshold. Margaret protested that she only wanted to honour and exalt a holy place; but she had hardly reached the hallway when suddenly her whole body was seized with excruciating torments:

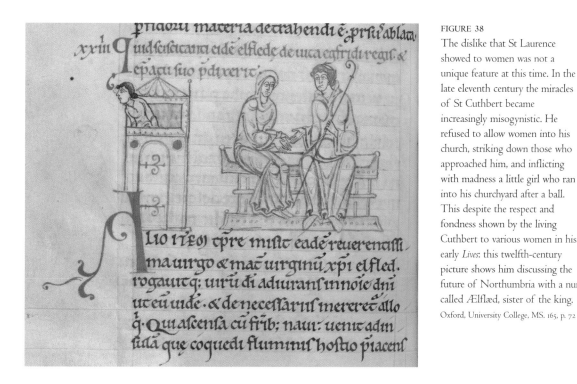

FIGURE 38

The dislike that St Laurence showed to women was not a unique feature at this time. In the late eleventh century the miracles of St Cuthbert became increasingly misogynistic. He refused to allow women into his church, striking down those who approached him, and inflicting with madness a little girl who ran into his churchyard after a ball. This despite the respect and fondness shown by the living Cuthbert to various women in his early *Lives*: this twelfth-century picture shows him discussing the future of Northumbria with a nun called Ælflæd, sister of the king.

Oxford, University College, MS. 165, p. 72

'Quickly', she cried out, *'take me away from here: see, I am dying now.'*

The clerks carried her away and prayed for her until she was better, and then she gave the church a silver cross and chalice, among other gifts. This was written probably *circa* 1091, so before Margaret's death in 1093. It shows that Margaret's reputation for religious zeal was upheld as far south as Canterbury, even if her sex did not commend her to St Laurence. Interestingly, according to the thirteenth-century collection of Margaret's posthumous miracles she once healed a young woman who had been struck down for carding wool on St Laurence's eve.

Turgot's Life

Our main source for Margaret's adult life is the biography which contains the story of the Gospel-book's rescue from the river.[16] It was written probably about ten years after her death, and was commissioned by her daughter Edith-Matilda, who became queen of England in 1100 when she married Henry I. Edith-Matilda had spent much of her youth far away from the Scottish court being educated at Wilton Abbey in Wessex; the author describes her wish that:

even though you only knew your mother's outward appearance slightly, you may have a full account of her virtues.

The author of the *Life* says that he was Margaret's chaplain for many years and knew her well, and it is likely that he was a monk called Turgot, prior of Durham, who spent some time as Margaret's chaplain. Margaret's son, King Alexander I, helped get Turgot appointed as bishop of St Andrews in 1107, but he later retired back to Durham, and died there in 1115. However, there are a few reasons why we cannot be certain that he was the author of the *Life*: for one thing one of the surviving manuscripts of the Life names the author as 'Theodore'. (But for ease of reference I shall refer to the author as Turgot in this book.)

Turgot did not write Margaret's *Life* in the way a modern audience would expect; although he says that Margaret told him the whole story of her life until they were both weeping too much to speak, he does not mention her birth in exile or her mother's connections, or anything at all about the practical aspects of her life before she became queen. There are two reasons for this. First, Turgot is writing a spiritual biography, in which Margaret's virtues and beliefs are more significant than the events of her life; secondly, he is writing for her daughter, Edith-Matilda, who had herself recently been elevated to the rank of queen through her marriage to Henry I. There was a particular genre of writing in the Middle Ages known as 'a mirror for princes' which was intended to inspire rulers to govern well by setting before them a good example. Turgot is writing a mirror for a princess. He is trying to show Edith-Matilda how her mother carried out her duties as queen; he tells her how Margaret used to talk to her young children, even though Edith-Matilda would presumably remember this, because he wants to remind her to bring her own children up similarly. He claims to be doing this at Margaret's own request, shortly before she died:

> I ask of you … that you will be the caretaker of my sons and daughters, and particularly that you give them love. You will teach them to love and fear God, and you will never cease teaching them, and whenever you see one of them exalted to the summit of earthly dignity, you will approach that one especially as a father and a teacher.

Turgot's description of his relationship with Margaret is rather touching; she told him so much about herself not because there was anything good in him, he explains, but because she thought there was.

FIGURE 39
St Edith, the elder sister of King Æthelred the Unready, was Margaret's great-great-aunt, and shared with her a sense of appropriate dress. She was famously rebuked by St Æthelwold for wearing robes which he thought rather too grand, but was uncowed by this, replying that God saw through outer things into the inner person, and that she could be just as holy in fine clothes as in a goatskin. According to her later hagiographer Edith was offered the throne instead of Æthelred after the murder of their brother, Edward king and martyr, but refused it in order to remain a nun at Wilton, where she spent her entire short life of twenty-three years.[17] Edith was famously learned, and was taught by two Continental priests employed for that purpose by her doting father, King Edgar the Peacemaker. She was said to have 'sweet eloquence, a noble intellect capable in all kinds of thought, a perceptive ardour in reading, hands as elegant as they were accomplished in painting and in writing as scribe or as author'. We know that she made at least one book at Wilton. She also had her own seal, pictured here, describing her as 'Royal Sister', so presumably made after her brother Edward succeeded to the throne in 975.
London, British Library, MS. Harley Ch. 45 A. 36, seal

MARGARET'S SPIRITUALITY

Turgot describes Margaret's spirituality as threefold in nature:

Zealous in sacred reading, persistent in prayer, unflagging in compassion, she carefully kept herself totally occupied in all things which were of God.

Learning, books and devotions

Turgot makes several references to Margaret's intelligence and her fondness for books. Her learnedness is the next thing he mentions about her after her illustrious ancestry. He says that she began to study in youth:

She had a keenly acute intellect for weighing up what she needed to understand, a tenacious memory for recalling many things, and a happy facility for expressing them in words.

Turgot describes Margaret as arguing from 'the testimony of the Holy Scriptures or the opinions of the Fathers', and reports her quoting Gregory the Great. He talks of the great trouble to which he went to find books for her, suggesting that her interests stretched beyond the Gospels and the psalms, which must have been easily attainable.

Margaret was eleven years old when she first came to England with her family, so her very early education would have taken place in Hungary. Edward the Exile's children were probably taken under the care of Queen Edith after his death in 1057, and it is likely that the two girls, Margaret and Christina, spent some time at Wilton Abbey, near Salisbury. This nunnery had long had strong links with the West-Saxon royal family. Its patron saint, Edith, was the daughter of King Edgar the Peacemaker (957–75), Margaret's great-great-grandfather. Queen Edith, wife of Edward the Confessor, may have been named after this Edith; she was herself educated at Wilton, and later had parts of it rebuilt. She also seems to have retired there in her widowhood, and witnessed a land sale in an upper room there in 1072. After the Norman Conquest the association between Wilton and the English royalty and nobility continued: Gunnhild, Harold II's daughter, lived there; Margaret's sister, Christina, was a Wilton nun; and Margaret seems to have sent her daughters Edith-Matilda and Mary there for their education. Lanfranc describes Margaret as *regaliter educata*, educated as befits a royal. So it is likely that Margaret acquired her learning at Wilton, one of the foremost English centres of women's education.

Unfortunately not one single book survives which we know to have been at Wilton in the Anglo-Saxon period, and neither is there any book list or description of its teaching; but we do have descriptions of the learning of various women who were educated there. Queen Edith, sister of Harold II and wife of Edward the Confessor, was educated at Wilton and is said to

FIGURE 40
There is one surviving manuscript which may perhaps have been made at Anglo-Saxon Wilton; this is a late tenth-century psalter, written during the lifetime of St Edith. This initial 'N' shows a nun.
Salisbury, Cathedral Library, MS. 150, 60v

have been very learned: 'she diligently read religious and secular books, and excelled in the writing of prose and verse… She could speak the language used in Gaul, as well as Danish and Irish, as though they were her mother tongues'.[18] A Wilton nun called Eve lent books to the hagiographer Goscelin in the second half of the eleventh century. Muriel of Angers, a famous Latin poet, probably lived at Wilton in the early twelfth century and was buried there. Wilton was the only nunnery in England which contributed original Latin verses to the mortuary roll of Abbot Vitalis of Savigny, which circulated circa 1122–3. It seems that Latin learning flourished at Wilton during the eleventh century and beyond, so Turgot's description of Margaret's knowledge and love of learning is entirely plausible.

Margaret's learning was not a theoretical accomplishment, but one she used in debate over church practices and also, it seems from some of Turgot's remarks, in legal matters:

> I admire the fact that among the tumult of lawsuits, among the manifold cares of the kingdom, she worked hard with wonderful zeal at divine reading, which she used to debate with the most learned men of the kingdom sat beside her, asking subtle and wise questions. And just as no one among them was more profound in mental ability, so no one was more profound in eloquence. Usually it fell out that the wisest men themselves went away from her wiser than they had come.

Turgot describes how at the beginning of her reign she argued for three days with the leaders of the Scottish church about several matters of church observance, 'fighting with the sword of the spirit, that is the word of God'. King Malcolm himself acted as her interpreter from Old English to Gaelic, showing his confidence in his wife's judgement: Turgot's audience will have remembered Bede's story of how the saintly King Oswald of Northumbria had translated for the Irish bishop Aidan from Iona.[19]

Margaret's concern with religious observance and doctrine is often portrayed in modern writings either as mere pedantry or as cultural imperialism, but this is a very modern point of view of the things she debated. The exact date of the start of Lent may not seem a vital issue to us, but it is important to remember that people in the Middle Ages were much more alert than we are to symbolism and resonances, and had a more sophisticated connection with ceremonies and observance.

Margaret's two most important changes to the Scottish church were about observances relating to Easter. She found that the Scots did not start Lent at the same time as the rest

The famous debate in the seventh century over the date of Easter — settled at the Synod of Whitby in 664 under another important woman, the redoubtable St Hild — was about far more than the relative authority of the 'Celtic' and Roman churches. In the system of calculation followed by some of the Irish it was possible for the full moon of Easter to fall before the spring equinox. The Venerable Bede explains that it was at the spring equinox, when the light and dark of each day are equal and the light on the increase, that the world was created and the sun first placed in the sky.[20] The sun symbolizes Christ, the light of the world, and the moon, which shines only through the sun's reflected light, symbolizes the people of God, who can only be truly good through God's grace.

Therefore to celebrate Easter, the supreme feast of the Christian church, at a full moon before the spring equinox, that is at a time when the moon is in a more perfect state than the sun, is to state that man, by nature, is capable of achieving true goodness without God's grace. This was the error of Pelagius, an influential early British heretic.

of the Western church. Lent is a time of contemplation and penitence before the celebration of Easter, and lasts forty days because after his baptism Jesus spent forty days in the desert overcoming temptation before he started his ministry. (It is one of several symbolic periods of forty days in the Bible, such as the length of time that the Ark spent on the flood.) The Scottish were not starting Lent on Ash Wednesday, but on the Monday of the following week, and in this intermediate period while the rest of the church had entered into the solemn period of preparation for Easter they were still in normal time. The Scottish ecclesiastics argued that they observed forty-two days of fasting, but Margaret pointed out that the Sundays did not count, since they were already special days whether or not they fell in Lent, and that they were therefore only fasting for thirty-six days. (This is why Lent is actually longer than forty days.)

Margaret also found that the Scottish did not celebrate Holy Communion on Easter Day. The church leaders said this was because they did not think they were worthy to take it. The Eucharist, at which bread and wine are blessed and shared as the body of the risen Christ, is an important part of Christian observance, and a central part of the community of Christian believers; St Paul said, 'For we being many are one bread, and one body: for we are all partakers of that one bread' (I Corinthians 10: 17). It was instituted by Jesus at the Last Supper, and its message of communion in Christ's sacrifice and in his triumph is of particular relevance to Easter Day, when Christians celebrate the resurrection of Christ, his victory over death. Furthermore, to refuse to take communion because of unworthiness would be to imply, conversely, that it was possible to be worthy of it, that in some way one might 'deserve' Jesus' sacrifice and eternal life; thus there is an implication of denial, in refusing communion for this reason, of the pure gift of God's grace which lies behind the theology of the eucharist. Margaret argued that if sinners were not to take the sacrament, then no one could, and that therefore Holy Communion was not meant to be viewed in this way. She stressed the need for approaching it thoughtfully, after confession, penance, and charity, three activities particularly associated with Lent. If the people could not receive this gift, central to the Christian faith, on Easter day at the celebration of the Resurrection, when could they receive it?

Turgot stresses that Margaret countered these uncanonical observances on two grounds, 'by reason and by authority'; she not only showed reasons against the Scottish customs, but argued for the importance of shared observance for the unity of the wider church.

Margaret also imposed the observance of Sunday as a day when people could rest from their labours, quoting Gregory the Great, who had once reproved a man for working on Sunday but had excommunicated for two months the overseer who had ordered him to do it. After Margaret's rebuke no one would 'dare compel another person to do any work' on a Sunday. She defended the correct ritual for mass; Turgot is unable to give us any details about the ritual she

FIGURE 42

Turgot compares Margaret's triumph in religious debate to that of St Helena. Helena was believed to have been British, and in this he links Margaret to an earlier Celtic past. She was the mother of the emperor Constantine, who converted the Roman empire to Christianity after he had a vision of the cross in the sky before an important battle. Helena was held to have rediscovered the remains of the True Cross in Jerusalem, after a spirited debate with Jews there on the nature of Jesus. We know that Margaret had a special devotion to the Cross — she prayed the Hours of the Holy Cross regularly and had a favourite reliquary of the True Cross, called the Black Rood, which she had brought to her on her deathbed — so this reference to St Helena is doubly appropriate. Helena was the subject of an Old English poem, *Elene*, which describes her as 'the victory-queen … filled with the spirit of wisdom'.[21]

Oxford, Bodleian Library, MS. Lat. liturg. d. 42, 31r

suppressed, but again it shows Margaret imposing Catholic practice in this most important and resonant of all Christian celebrations. All these acts were not mere exercises of doctrinal pedantry, but were about caring for her people, charity in its true sense of neighbourly love: she encouraged them to take the Eucharist, sign of God's grace, on Easter Day, showing that it was a free gift rather than something to be earned; she defended the right of all people to spend Sundays on spiritual matters rather than be compelled to work; and in bringing the Scottish church's practices into line with those of Rome she helped her people enter more fully into a Christian fraternity that stretched across Europe.

Choice of Gospel-book texts

St Margaret's Gospel-book does not contain the whole of the four Gospels, but only extracts from them, presumably in order to make it a small, portable book. As such it attests more to literate piety than to learned reading. The extracts chosen are all prefaced by a short title saying which Gospel they are taken from, even though this information is redundant because the extracts are arranged in Gospel order. This suggests that the texts were copied from a Gospel-lectionary, a type of book in which the Gospel readings were copied out in the order in which they were read at church services through the course of the liturgical year. This choice of exemplar, and this way of labelling the texts in the manuscripts to point out their liturgical connection, suggests that the seasonal associations of the texts might have been just as important a factor in their selection as the contents of the texts themselves.

FIGURE 43

A picture of the evangelist St
Luke faces the start of his
Gospel. The opening words
of Luke, where he introduces
the work to Theophilus, have
no liturgical associations, and
must have been included so
that the normal decorative
scheme of a Gospel-book
could be followed.

Oxford, Bodleian Library, MS. Lat.
liturg. f. 5, 21v–22r

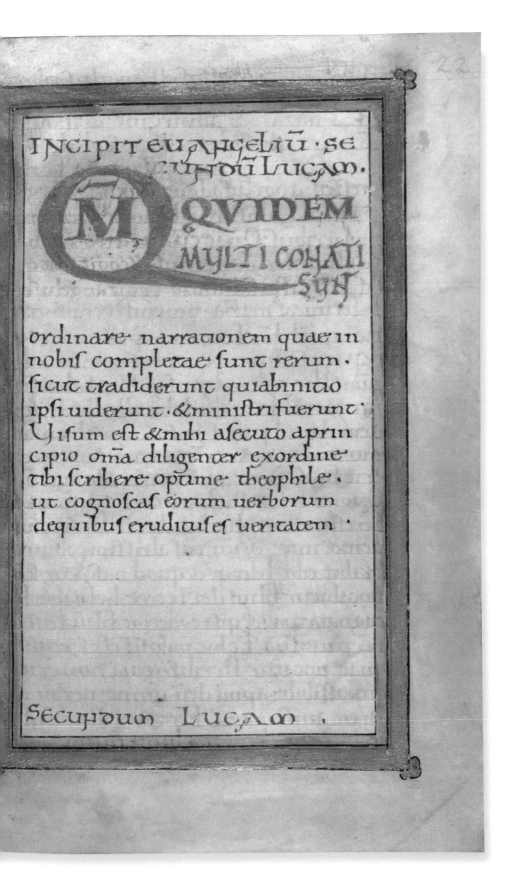

INCIPIT EUANGELIU · SE
CUNDU LUCAM ·

QM QUIDEM
MULTI CONATI
SUN

ordinare narrationem quae in
nobif completae funt rerum ·
ficut tradiderunt quiabinitio
ipfi uiderunt · &miniftri fuerunt ·
Uifum eft &mihi afecuto aprin
cipio omña diligenter exordine
tibi fcribere optime theophile ·
ut cognofcaf eorum uerborum
dequibuf erudituf ef ueritatem ·

SECUNDUM LUCAM ·

FIGURE 44

St Matthew the Evangelist and
the start of his Gospel, listing
the ancestors of Christ. This is
the only one of the Gospels in
St Margaret's Gospel-book
which starts with a decorated
letter. Because the *Liber
Generationis*, the genealogy of
Christ, has a special status the
'L' for *liber generationis* is usually
decorated in Gospel
manuscripts, often with the
same interlace and beast-head
finials as seen here. This type
of decoration has its origins
in an Insular style which was
exported to the Continent,
where it developed into what
was known as the Franco-
Saxon style before being
imported back to England.
Oxford, Bodleian Library, MS. Lat.
liturg. f. 5, 3v–4r

INCIPIT EUAN
GELIUM SCDM
MATTHEUM

LIBER
GENE
RATIO

nis ihu xpi filii dauid filii
Abraham. A braham autem ge
nuit isaac. isaac autem genuit ia
cob · Iacob autem genuit iudam
& fratres eius. iudas autem genuit
phares & zara dethamar · Phares
autem genuit esrom. esrom aut
genuit aram ·

All four Gospels have their opening texts, presumably to make it easy for the book to contain the usual decoration for a Gospel-book, that is evangelist portraits and decorated first words for each Gospel. All have the full Passion narratives, which were of course extremely important texts. In the selection of other texts we can see an interest in the Blessed Virgin Mary, which is not unusual at this period.[22] There is also an interest in the other women who were part of Jesus' ministry, like Mary Magdalen. The story of Mary and Martha is included, when Jesus said that Mary, in choosing to listen to him rather than do household work with Martha, had chosen the better part; this was an important text for nuns and other people devoted to the religious life. Matthew 20:17–19, a very short reading, is that set in two mid-eleventh-century Anglo-Saxon service-books as the Gospel for the weekly Mass of the Holy Cross, said on Saturdays. This could tie in with Margaret's devotion to the Holy Cross — we know this started while she was in England, if not earlier, since she took the Black Rood, her relic of the True Cross, with her to Scotland. So in these texts we can perhaps see the interests of Margaret, and it is tempting to think that this suggests that the book was made specially for her; but on the other hand these interests would not have been very unusual at the time.

The texts in St Margaret's Gospel-book: their contents and liturgical association

Matthew

1:1–21	The ancestry of Jesus: Christmas vigil (24 December)
2:1–12	The Magi: Epiphany (6 January)
3:13–17	The baptism of Christ: Epiphany (6 January) and the week after Epiphany
4:1–11	The temptation of Christ: the start of Lent
4:18–22	The calling of the fishermen: St Andrew's day (30 November)
20:17–19	Jesus predicts his death and Resurrection: Saturday's weekly Mass of the Holy Cross
26:2–28:7	A woman (later identified with Mary Magdalen) anoints Jesus' feet; the Last Supper; the Mount of Olives; the Passion; the burial; the Marys at the tomb: Holy Week
28:16–20	The Great Commission: Easter Week

Mark

1:1–8	John the Baptist preaches in the desert: the start of Advent
6:17–29	The beheading of John the Baptist: the feast of the beheading of John the Baptist (29 August)
14:1–15:46	A woman anoints Jesus' feet; the Last Supper; the Mount of Olives; the passion; the burial: Holy Week

16:1–7	The Marys at the tomb: Easter Day
16:14–20	Jesus appears to the disciples; his ascension: Ascension Sunday
Luke	
1:1–4	Luke introduces his work to Theophilus: no liturgical association
1:26–38	Gabriel announces Jesus' birth to Mary (including the *Magnificat*): the Annunciation (25 March) and the week before Christmas
2:1–14	The Nativity: Christmas Day (25 December)
2:21	The circumcision and naming of Christ: the feast of the circumcision of Christ (1 January)
2:22–32	The presentation of Christ in the temple (including *Nunc Dimittis*): the Purification of the Virgin Mary (2 February)
10:38–42	Mary and Martha: many liturgical associations, including the Assumption of the Virgin Mary (15 August)

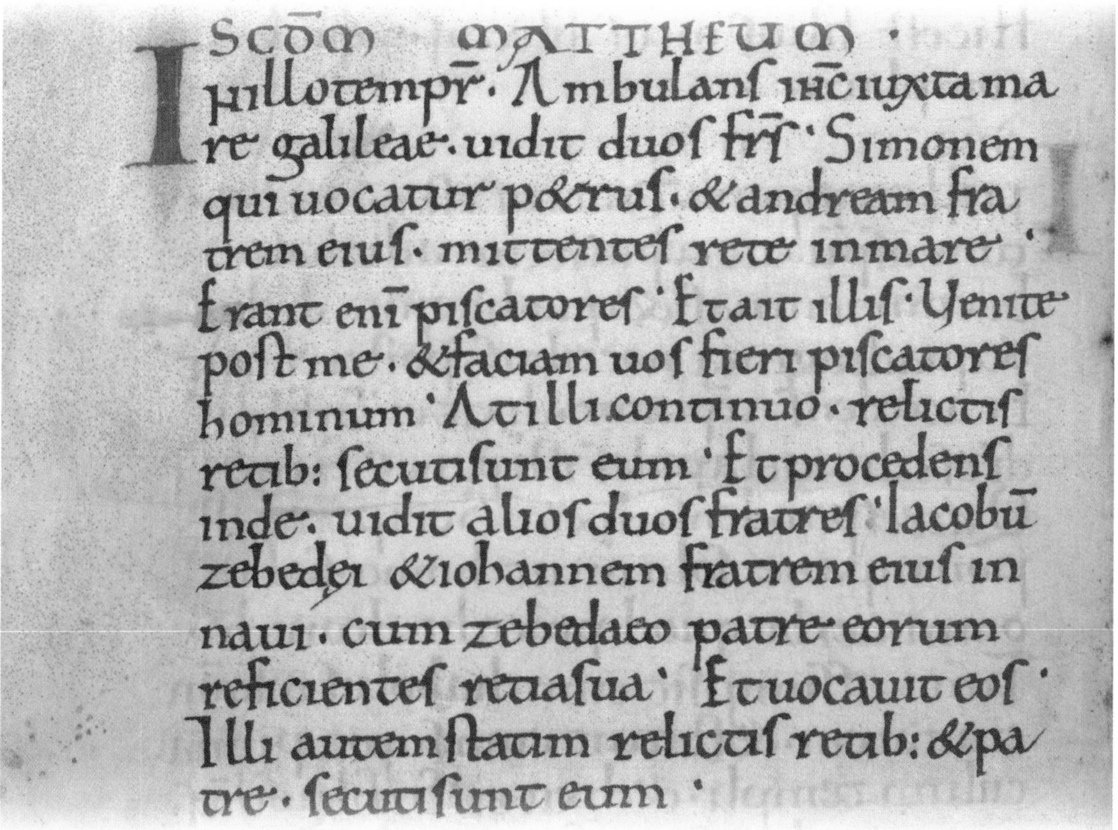
SCDM MATTHEUM ·
In illo tempr. Ambulans ihc iuxta ma
re galileae. uidit duos frs. Simonem
qui uocatur petrus. & andream fra
trem eius. mittentes rete inmare.
Erant enim piscatores. Et ait illis. Uenite
post me. & faciam uos fieri piscatores
hominum. At illi continuo. relictis
retib: secutisunt eum. Et procedens
inde. uidit alios duos fratres. Iacobū
zebedei & iohannem fratrem eius in
naui. cum zebedaeo patre eorum
reficientes retiasua. Et uocauit eos.
Illi autem statim relictis retib: & pa
tre. secuti sunt eum.

FIGURE 45
St Andrew, brother of Peter, was one of the most popular apostles and had associations with a number of places as well as Scotland. An Old English poem survives about St Andrew's missionary work after Jesus' ascension; it uses heroic terms which perhaps deliberately parallel him with the great pagan warrior Beowulf.[21]
Oxford, Bodleian Library, MS. Lat. liturg. f. 5, 6v

Matthew 4: 18–22
And Jesus, walking by the sea of Galilee, saw two brethren, Simon called Peter, and Andrew his brother, casting a net into the sea: for they were fishers. And he saith unto them, Follow me, and I will make you fishers of men.

FIGURE 46
The illustration in the Book of Deer is sometimes criticised for naivety, but its almost abstract figures have a powerful simplicity. This picture shows two evangelists, with book satchels on straps round their necks, and two angels above them. This image is at the start of the book, and there is another similar at the end, so that the whole book is framed by the evangelists and angels.
Cambridge, University Library, MS. Ii. 6. 32, iv

22:1–23:53	The Last Supper; the Mount of Olives; the Passion; the deposition: Holy Week
24:1–12	The Marys and Peter see the empty tomb: the second week after Easter

John

1:1–14	John's statement of the theology of the Incarnation: Christmas Day (25 December)
14:23–31	Jesus talks of his leaving and the sending of the Holy Spirit: Pentecost
17:1–11	Jesus prays about his witness, and for his disciples, before his death: the fifth week of Lent, and Ascension vigil
18:1–19:42	The betrayal in the garden; the Passion; the burial: Maundy Thursday
20:1–9	Mary Magdalen, John, and Peter see the empty tomb: Easter Saturday

There are six eleventh-century Anglo-Saxon Gospel-books containing extracts rather than the whole texts. It is interesting to note that five of these left England – apart from St Margaret's in Scotland, three went early to Germany (two of these are now in New York) and one is in Poland. Probably this sort of book was usually the personal possession of the type of important people who were prone to political exile or arranged overseas marriages. The three that went to Germany are associated with Judith of Flanders, wife of Earl Tostig.[24] (She also owned a surviving complete Gospel-book.) They were written in the 1050s or early 1060s (though at least some of the work may have been done after her flight to the continent in 1065); they are therefore contemporary with Margaret's book. Only one of the six surviving Anglo-Saxon Gospel-lectionaries of this type remained in England; this manuscript is also from the middle of the eleventh century. We do not know in what circumstances it was made, but it seems to have been at Hereford or Worcester Cathedral by the end of the century (see Figs. 18 and 24).

The only surviving pre-Norman book from Scotland is also a volume of Gospel extracts, known as the Book of Deer (see Fig. 46).[25] It was written in the middle of the tenth century, and was at Deer in Aberdeenshire in the eleventh century. It is a descendant of the Irish tradition of personal pocket Gospel-books, which were written sometimes in tiny script to make them easily portable. By including only extracts rather than the full Gospels it was possible to have a portable book which was also more legible and decorative. The use and original ownership of the Book of Deer is a mystery; its extracts may have had medical associations.

We know from texts that there must have been a lot of little private books in Anglo-Saxon England which do not survive to us. King Alfred the

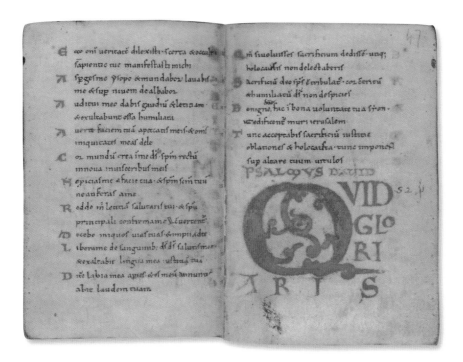

Great had his own little commonplace book, and St Edith copied out a selection of devotional texts at Wilton at the end of the tenth century. Although most of such materials are lost to us we can still see a few remnants, such as the little prayerbook of Ælfwine, dean of the New Minster, Winchester, or the tiny Anglo-Saxon Psalter now in the Bodleian.

There is one other surviving book which may have been owned by St Margaret, a psalter now in Edinburgh University Library.[26] We can tell from the script that this psalter was written in Ireland or Scotland in the eleventh century, but there is no way of telling on which side of the Irish Sea it originated. At the end of the eleventh century one of the decorated pages was erased and repainted in an Anglo-Saxon style. We know that the manuscript was in Scotland by the first half of the sixteenth century. If it was written in Scotland, then it would be very tempting to assume that the illumination in Anglo-Saxon style was done in Scotland by someone in Margaret's circle. However, the book could equally have been written in Ireland and the Anglo-Saxon decoration added in England — there are other examples of Irish books that were imported to southern England in the late Anglo-Saxon period, and had their decoration altered there — in which case the manuscript probably travelled to Scotland much later. Medieval manuscripts did move about rather more than they are given credit for, so the ownership of this manuscript by Margaret must remain just a possibility.

FIGURE 47 *above*
This little psalter, shown here at actual size, is roughly contemporary with St Margaret's Gospel-book. The script is tiny, and the book quite thick, making it possible to include the whole psalter and some private prayers without the need for excerpting the texts.
Oxford, Bodleian Library, MS. Laud lat. 81, 46v-47r

FIGURE 48 *right*
This illustration shows the repainted opening to Psalm 52, *Quid gloriaris in malitia*. This is in an Anglo-Saxon style and replaced an original Celtic decorated page of which only the interlace at the corners survives. The next opening is in the original style, with interlace decoration and Insular script.
Edinburgh, University Library, MS. 56, 50r

QUID GLORIARIS in malicia qui potens es in iniquitate.

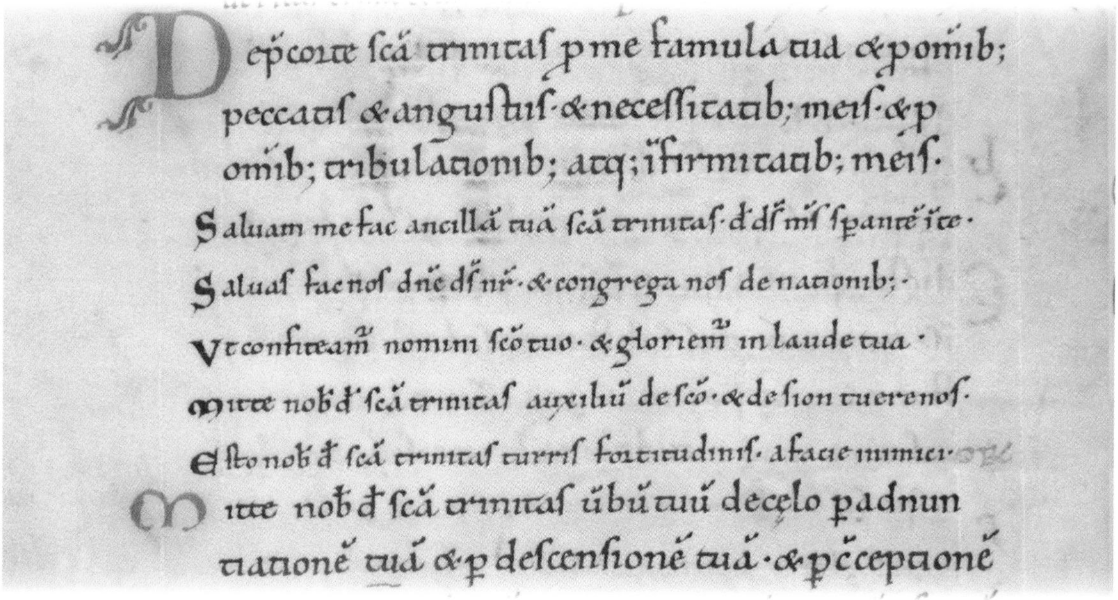

epcoite sca trinitas p me famula tua &pomib;
peccatis &angustiis·&necessitatib; meis·&p
omib; tribulationib; atq; ifirmitatib; meis·
Saluam me fac ancillā tuā scā trinitas·d̄ d̄s m̄s spatiē ite·
Saluas fac nos d̄ne d̄s n̄r·&congrega nos de nationib;·
Vt confiteam nomini scō tuo·&gloriem̄ in laude tua·
Mitte nob d̄ scā trinitas auxiliū de scō·&de sion tuere nos·
Esto nob d̄ scā trinitas turris fortitudinis·a facie inimici·
Mitte nob d̄ scā trinitas ūbū tuū de cęlo padnun
tiatione tuā &p descensione tuā·&pceptione

FIGURE 49

The Crowland Psalter did not remain at
St Guthlac's Abbey for long: in the early
twelfth century it was at Lewes, a
Cluniac house in Sussex, where an obit
of a prior who died in 1107 was added.
Crowland lost muniments and books in
a disastrous fire of 1091, so probably the
Psalter had already left by this point —
it may have been alienated in the
political turmoils
after the Norman Conquest.

One clue to its intermediate
whereabouts can be found in an added
text, a daily round of services of
devotion to the Holy Trinity, adapted
for private use and with phrases such as
famula tua, your servant, in the feminine
form. This suggests that the manuscript
was used by a woman for private
devotion in the late eleventh century.

The Cluniac monastery at Lewes
was founded by William de Warenne
and his wife, Gundrada; she was from a
noble Flemish family who had probably
already had estates in England before
the Norman Conquest. They had links
with the east of England: Gundrada
owned land there in the right of her
brother Frederick, who had been
murdered by Hereward the Wake, and
William, who also had large estates
there, was involved in putting down
local English rebellions against the
Conqueror. Gundreda was buried at
Lewes, and her epitaph survives there
on a memorial slab, with details of her
noble birth and great personal piety. So
although we cannot be certain, one
possibility is that the Crowland Psalter
was owned by Gundrada and the
services added for her use. This office
is probably quite close to the one
Margaret used.

Oxford, Bodleian Library, MS. Douce 296, 129v

Worship and prayer

Turgot says that Margaret engaged from a young age in *lectio divina*, divine reading, a monastic practice of meditative engagement with holy texts. It is probably in this context that she would have used her little Gospel-book. It is small enough to have been easily carried around for use in private moments or when her usual routine was disrupted.

Turgot also describes Margaret's routine of prayer and worship during the two strictest times of the year, Lent and the forty days before Christmas. She would get up in the night to say the Lauds of the Holy Trinity, the Holy Cross, and the Virgin Mary. She then said the Offices of the Dead and the whole psalter. Next she and Malcolm washed the feet of six paupers and gave them alms. After another period of sleep she would sing psalms while feeding nine baby orphans, whom she sat in her lap and fed with specially-prepared soft food from her own spoons. Then she and the king would hold a feast for three hundred paupers, whom they would serve themselves. Margaret then returned to church to pray the rest of the Hours of the Holy Trinity, the Holy Cross, and the Virgin Mary, as well as further Psalms. At the evening meal she fed twenty-four paupers before herself; according to Turgot these twenty-four stayed with her through all the year, travelling with her.

It is interesting to note quite how intrinsic a part of Margaret's liturgical round was the feeding and serving of the poor. Twice Turgot refers to her 'serving Christ in these paupers'; the acts of worship and charity were inseparable for her. This perhaps shows influence from the Benedictine injunction that all people must be approached as if they were Christ. Foot-washing was a common part of liturgical practice in the Middle Ages, because Jesus washed his disciples' feet at the Last Supper; it lies behind the surviving tradition that the monarch should give special alms to a group of pensioners on Maundy Thursday.

Margaret did three sets of Hours in these intense periods of the year, the Hours of the Holy Trinity, Holy Cross, and Virgin Mary. These would have consisted of a series of short services or 'offices' for each of the monastic hours, which could be said alone and outside church. (The same choice of Hours is found in the little private prayerbook made in the 1020s for Ælfwine, the dean of the New Minster at Winchester, though in a basic form with only one office for each.)[27] In the later medieval period all noble or genteel women would have their Book of Hours of the Virgin, and in the devotions of Margaret we can see a forerunner of this.

It is interesting that each of these sets of Hours is addressed to a feminine recipient. The Holy Trinity, *sancta trinitas*, is feminine in Latin, and in the surviving texts of the Hours of the Holy Trinity from Anglo-Saxon England there are therefore prayers to the *creatrix* rather than the creator, the *gubernatrix* (governor), and *adiutrix* (helper), all in the feminine form. The

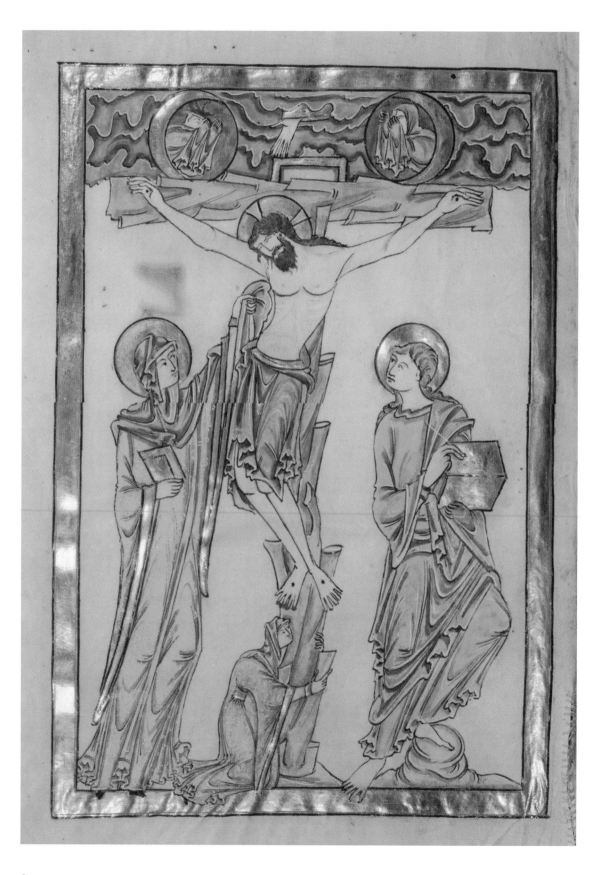

FIGURE 50 *left*
Countess Judith of Flanders, sister-in-law of Harold II and cousin of Edward the Confessor, clings to the cross. The Virgin Mary, carrying a book, holds her blue mantle up to Jesus' wounds, while John the Evangelist writes his Gospel. In the sky the sun and moon cover their faces in grief, symbolizing the darkness at the death of Christ, and the hand of God extends in blessing. Judith's pose may suggest a special devotion to the Holy Cross, like Margaret's. In its style and palette this illumination is a useful comparandum for St Margaret's Gospel-book. It was probably made in the 1050s or early 1060s.

New York, Pierpont Morgan, MS. M. 709, IV

FIGURE 51 *above*
A noblewoman venerates the virgin. This is probably a picture of Matilda of Tuscany, a prominent Continental heiress, later Judith of Flanders' daughter-in-law. She had substantial military power in her own right, and was the chief supporter of Pope Gregory in his battle against Emperor Henry IV

Oxford, Bodleian Library, MS. Auct. D. 2. 6, 158v.

Holy Cross, *sancta crux*, is also female, and so, of course, is the Virgin Mary. But for Margaret the Virgin Mary was not the first choice in order to address prayers to a feminine recipient.

Charity and Queenship
Paupers, pilgrims and monks

Margaret's name means pearl. Turgot comments on how fitting this was:

> she was a precious pearl in the sight of God because of her faith and good works ... Let others admire in others tokens of miracles; in Margaret I admire much more the works of compassion.

Her charitable work did not cease outside the liturgy. Turgot talks of her role as mother of her people: when she rode out, orphans and widows would come to her for alms, and if she ran out her retainers would happily supply her, knowing they would be generously reimbursed. She engaged in some very practical works of charity: she sent out her servants to find and ransom English people who had been enslaved after the turmoil of the Norman Conquest; and she set up lodging houses with servants and a ferry across the Firth of Forth for the large number of pilgrims who visited St Andrew's.

Soon after becoming queen she built a church at Dunfermline, the place where she had married Malcolm. She decorated it lavishly with objects including a gold and silver jewelled cross which was still there when Turgot wrote. She also set up a monastic community there, with the help of Lanfranc, archbishop of Canterbury. In the Middle Ages monks and nuns often looked after the poor and the unwell for whom there was little other provision. As well as importing monks from the south, she also visited and supported the culdees, ascetic hermits in an ancient Gaelic tradition, whose name comes from the Old Irish *Céle Dé*, or companions of God. Often they would refuse to accept the gifts she offered; instead she would ask them to suggest works of charity that she could carry out on their behalf.

Like St Edith of Wilton, Margaret engaged in embroidery for liturgical uses. She had a kind of embroidery workshop in her chambers, where noble women made decorated vestments for priests. To avoid scandal only well-behaved women were chosen to work with her, and no men were allowed unless the queen was present.

Malcolm and their family

Margaret also seems to have believed it her duty as queen to uphold the dignity and splendour of the royal court. She made Malcolm dress appropriately for a king and compelled his courtiers to dress splendidly too, in decorated multicoloured fabrics. (Later claims that she invented the tartan are not convincing.) She increased Malcolm's retinue when he rode out, but was careful to ensure that this band was kept under control and not allowed to harass ordinary people. She redecorated the royal hall and bought gold and silver tableware. The *Anglo-Saxon Chronicle* describes how when Edgar the Ætheling left Scotland for France in 1075 she and Margaret loaded him and his men with:

> many gifts and treasures in furs covered with rich cloth, and in robes of marten-fur and miniver-fur and ermine-fur and in rich cloth, and in gold and silver vessels.

In later tradition Margaret was supposed to have invented the loving-cup, where a large drinking vessel is passed around all the guests at a feast, and everyone drinks in turn with gestures of mutual respect. This is still done in some place, for example Oxford and Cambridge colleges and ancient London guilds.

Unlucky as ever, Edgar lost it all in a shipwreck, but Malcolm and Margaret replaced it before sending him off to make peace with the Normans. According to Turgot, she engaged in this splendour for the sake of royal dignity, while aware that under the gems and gold she was 'nothing but dust and ashes'.

Margaret's marriage may not have been of her choosing, but from the contemporary sources it seems she was widely held to have been a good influence on her husband — although there is often an element of a patronizing attitude to Scottish 'barbaric' culture in this. Turgot paints a picture of a loving couple, with Malcolm doting on his valued wife, kissing the books which he had seen were her favourites, even though he could not read, and sharing jokes with her:

> anything she rejected he also rejected, and anything she loved, he loved because of his desire for her love.

She seems to have been far from inactive in the kingdom:

> all things which were fitting were carried out by order of the prudent queen: by her counsel the laws of the kingdom were put in order; divine religion was augmented by her industry; and the people rejoiced in the prosperity of affairs... She made the king himself more obedient to justice, compassion, charity, and good works.

Margaret and Malcolm had at least eight children who survived to adulthood; six sons and two daughters. Their sons were called Edward, Edmund, Æthelred, Edgar, Alexander, and David, and their daughters Edith and Mary. (There may have been further daughters, because Edith later gave land to Durham for the souls of her deceased parents, brothers, and sisters; perhaps Edith and Mary are the only ones recorded because they went on to make important marriages.) It is notable that none of Margaret and Malcolm's children were given Gaelic names. Their first four sons were, in fact, named

Turgot tells the endearing story of how Margaret, if she ran out of money to give to the poor, would raid a store which Malcolm set aside to distribute as alms. Malcolm would sometimes lead Margaret before Turgot, her chaplain, joking that he had caught her red-handed, and demanding judgement. This is probably a reference by Malcolm to the Old English technical law term 'infangthief', trying a thief caught with the goods in his possession.

after Margaret's paternal ancestors, Edward the Exile, King Edmund Ironside, King Æthelred the Unready, and King Edgar the Peacemaker. (Alternatively they could be named after four of the last Anglo-Saxon kings of England, in which case Edward would be named for Edward the Confessor.) This is a very clear assertion of the value the couple placed on Margaret's English royal ancestry. Their daughter Edith may have been named after Edward the Confessor's wife, who probably took care of Margaret and her siblings after the death of their father; or perhaps after Margaret's great-great-aunt St Edith, sister of Æthelred the Unready, the patron saint of Wilton where Margaret was probably educated. (Edith was later to change her name to Matilda.)

According to Turgot, Margaret used to urge her children to the love of God, using words suitable to their ages. They were apparently so well-behaved that the younger ones always showed respect to the elder and they never fought amongst themselves: at mass they all went up to receive in order of their ages. Before she died she commended them to Turgot's care. However, her daughters in particular probably did not remain with Margaret for long; if Edith-Matilda went to Wilton with her aunt Christina in 1086 then she left Scotland when only about six years old.

FIGURE 52

Throughout much of the Middle Ages, English embroidery (*opus Anglicana*) was renowned for its high quality. From the early Anglo-Saxon period there was a strong tradition of making and giving of embroidered work to churches. These were presumably usually religious works, although we also know that the widow of Byrhtnoth of Essex gave tapestries to Ely, after his death fighting the Vikings in 991, which showed her husband's valorous deeds. (Ironically, the only major surviving example of this Anglo-Saxon habit is the Bayeux Tapestry, that great record of the end of Anglo-Saxon England, made probably at Canterbury in the decade or so after 1066.) St Edith of Wilton made vestments for priests, including one in which she portrayed herself as Mary Magdalen prostrate at the feet of Christ. This example is a maniple from the shrine of St Cuthbert, and shows St Peter the Deacon, disciple and friend of Gregory the Great. It was made between 909 and 916 at the command of Queen Ælfflæd, wife of King Edward the Elder, for Bishop Frithestan of Winchester.

St Cuthbert's maniple, Durham Cathedral Treasury

Margaret's legend, and her Gospel-book's fate

WHEN MARGARET DIED on 16 November 1093 she was only forty-six. She had been ill for some time, Turgot tells us, worn out with fasting (and perhaps also from so many pregnancies). While Margaret lay on her deathbed her husband, with some of their sons, was away raiding Anglo-Norman Northumbria, in retaliation for a calculated insult from William Rufus. Her fourth son, Edgar, was still in his teens; he returned home from the battle to find his mother sunk into her last hours of illness, praying Psalm 51 ('Have mercy on me, O God, according to thy loving-kindness') and revering her much-loved reliquary, the Black Rood. At first he tried to hide the truth from her, but when she questioned him repeatedly he admitted that both Malcolm and her oldest son, Edward, the designated heir, had been killed in battle with Robert de Mowbray, earl of Northumbria, a few days before. Margaret died shortly afterwards, praying in words taken from the liturgy of Holy Communion.

WHAT HAPPENED TO MARGARET'S BOOKS? Reginald of Durham, writing in the second half of the twelfth century, said that Margaret 'had beautifully decorated the shrine of St Cuthbert with many ornaments', including a silver Gospel-book and the cross which she was holding in her hands when she died.[28] (The cross was still at Durham in 1383, by which time it had been joined by Margaret's Black Rood; but this silver Gospel-book is not mentioned in the 1383 relic list.)[29] Scholars have in the past identified the silver Gospel-book with St Margaret's Gospel-book in the Bodleian, but there is no strong reason to believe this is the case. A *textus argenteus*, a silver Gospel-book, would have either been written in silver letters or, more probably, have had a silver treasure binding. Neither of these corresponds with the Bodleian manuscript, which according to Turgot had a gold and jewelled treasure binding. Furthermore the term *textus*, usually translated 'Gospel-book', implies something more authoritative than the slender and personal collection of excerpts in the Bodleian manuscript. Margaret must have had more than one Gospel-book — her contemporary Judith, wife of Earl Tostig, had at least four, and we would expect Margaret to have owned a complete copy of the Gospels — and since Reginald of Durham's description does not fit well with Turgot's description or the evidence of the surviving book, it was probably another of Margaret's manuscripts which went to Durham.

What happened after Margaret's death to the little Gospel-book now in the Bodleian is therefore a matter of conjecture; given her wide connections it could have gone to any number of places. Margaret had links with many monasteries in Scotland and England, including Durham, to which it could have been sent, or it could have gone to her burial place, Dunfermline, and later been attached to her shrine as Cuthbert's little Gospel of St John became attached to his. If it went to a member of her family then it could have gone to Dunkeld with her son Æthelred or to Montacute in Somerset with her penitent son Edmund. It could have gone to Boulogne with Mary, or passed down with the Scottish crown's possessions like the Black Rood. If Margaret's eldest daughter, Edith-Matilda, had inherited it then it could have easily ended up in London at her foundation of the Holy Trinity in Aldgate. (Given that it is next heard of in the possession of a resident of this parish, the antiquary John Stow, it is rather tempting to see this as the least complicated solution.)

We know rather more about what happened to Margaret's prized reliquary of the True Cross, known as the Black Rood. This was a black, perhaps ebony, case about an ell long: a Scottish ell is roughly equivalent to a metre, and an English ell rather longer, but at this date it might simply mean an arm's length. The case was decorated with gold and contained an ivory crucifix and a relic of the True Cross, also ornamented with gold. Margaret had brought it with her to Scotland; it was probably made in England, but perhaps it had come with Edward the Exile's family from Hungary in 1057. This reliquary stayed in the possession of the Scottish crown, and in 1153 Margaret's son David venerated it on his deathbed, just she had sixty years earlier. In 1291 it was one of the treasures captured by the English at the same time as the Stone of Scone; it was returned to the Scottish in 1328 (unlike the Stone, which was promised then but not delivered until 1996). In 1346 it was captured by the English again, along with the Scottish king David II, and this time the Black Rood went to the church of Durham, where it is recorded in the relic list of 1383. It was probably destroyed or plundered in the religious upheavals of the Reformation or the Commonwealth.

THE FATES OF HER CHILDREN

In November 1093 Margaret and Malcolm's children lost their father, their mother, and their oldest full-brother, all within the space of a few days. They were left in a difficult position. The succession to the kingship of Scotland was contested between Malcolm's younger brother, Domnall (Donald), and his oldest son, Donnchad (Duncan), child of his first wife Ingebjørg. Back during the reign of Macbeth when Malcolm had fled to England, Domnall Bàn (Shakespeare's Donaldbane) had taken refuge with their Gaelic kin in the west. He represented a growing group in the Scottish kingdom who resented the strong English influence over Scotland in Malcolm's reign (which had started even before Margaret's arrival), and who wanted a return to traditional Gaelic culture. In the contest over the succession Margaret's children were a side issue, representative to many of a disliked trend in recent history. It seems that Edgar the Ætheling, Margaret's brother, took charge of the younger children — one later legend even has him staging a raid to rescue Margaret's body from Edinburgh Castle where she died.

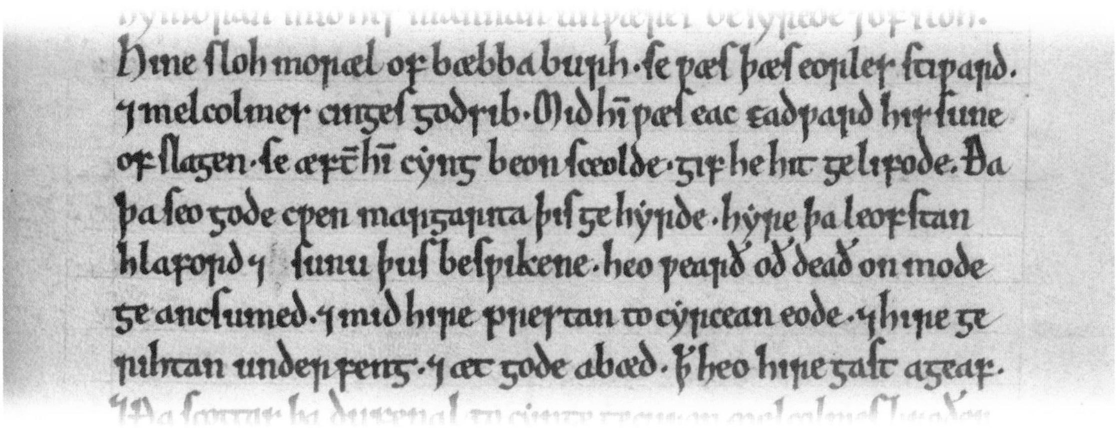
Hine sloh Moræl of bæbbaburh. se wæs þæs eorles stiward.
7 melcolmes cinges godsib. Mid hī wæs eac eadward his sune
of slagen. se æft hī cyng beon sceolde. gif he hit gelifode. Ða
þa seo gode cwen margarita þis gehyrde. hyre þa leofstan
hlaford 7 sunu þus beswikene. heo wearð oð deað on mode
geancsumed. 7 mid hire preostan to cyrcean eode. 7 hire ge
rihtan underfeng. 7 æt gode abæd. þ heo hire gast ageaf.

FIGURE 54

Although people often talk about 'The Anglo-Saxon Chronicle', in fact there are several different versions of the *Chronicle*. Eight manuscripts survive, related to each other in complicated ways; it seems that once the original *Chronicle* was written, probably at the court of King Alfred the Great (871–99), individual houses would add their own annals or acquire a new manuscript copied from another centre's work. The version with the most about Margaret is known as the D-chronicle, and is now in the British Library. It seems to have been written at Worcester or York, and incorporates northern material. The death of Margaret and that of her husband and son is told in the E-version of the *Anglo-Saxon Chronicle*, shown here. It emphasises that both Domnall and Donnchad were only accepted as kings when they had agreed to the exclusion of the English and French from Scotland. Margaret's children, with their English names and Norman connections, were no longer likely to be welcome in their homeland.[31]

Oxford, Bodleian Library, MS. Laud misc. 636, 69r

The Scots first chose Domnall as their king, driving out all the English who had been with Malcolm. Donnchad, Malcolm's oldest son, had been taken to England as a Norman hostage in 1072 when he was just a child, and he had chosen to stay there after his release in 1087; he now obtained King William Rufus' support to return to Scotland and fight for his inheritance. Donnchad was briefly accepted as king in 1094 on condition that he never again introduced Englishmen or Frenchmen into the country, but he was killed later that same year. Domnall now returned to the throne. Edmund, Margaret's oldest surviving son, had thrown his lot in with the Gaelicising party and he became associated in rule with his uncle Domnall, perhaps as his designated heir since Domnall had no son. In this Edmund seems to have alienated the rest of his family; he became known to posterity as the only bad child of Margaret, and was held to have been implicated in the death of his half-brother Donnchad. Æthelred, the next oldest of Margaret's sons, at some point became abbot of Dunkeld; it is probable that by the time of his parents' death he had already chosen the religious life, and this seems to have removed him from the succession. William Rufus transferred his support to the claims of Margaret's fourth son, Edgar, sending Margaret's brother Edgar the Ætheling with an army to fight against Domnall. In 1097 Domnall and Edmund were captured and deprived of the kingdom. Domnall was blinded. Edmund, after a period of imprisonment, became a Cluniac monk at Montacute in Somerset, and asked to be buried in his chains as a sign of his penitence.

Edgar now acceded to the throne. He patronized religious communities and made a very large donation to St Cuthbert at Durham; Aelred of Rievaulx likened him to his illustrious kinsman Edward the Confessor. When he died in 1107, after ten years on the throne, he was buried at Dunfermline with Margaret and Malcolm; as far away as Bury St Edmunds in Suffolk it was recorded that on that day 'God placed King Edgar above the stars'.[30]

'Good queen Maud' and the green branch

It is not clear where the daughters, Edith and Mary, were at the time of their parents' death. Edith was only twelve or thirteen and Mary younger. They had certainly already spent some years at Wilton Abbey, but their father had probably fetched them away from there in 1093, worried that they were likely to take the veil and be unavailable to secure future alliances by marriage. The girls seem to have been back at Wilton again in the late eleventh century. At some point Edith changed her name to Matilda, perhaps in honour of her godmother, Queen Matilda, William the Conqueror's queen who had died in 1083. (Edith-Matilda was also known as Maud, a contemporary variant of Matilda.)

In 1100 when William Rufus died in a hunting accident in the New Forest (the second of the Conqueror's sons to die in

This picture of Mary Magdalen in an early collection of Anselm's letters shows her veiled like a nun. Archbishop Anselm thought that, by occasionally being seen wearing a veil as a youth, Edith-Matilda had effectively taken nun's vows, something which she vehemently denied. She wrote to Anselm explaining that the veil had been put on her against her wishes by the abbess of the nunnery where she was staying, to protect her from the lascivious gaze of Norman nobles when they visited. Edith-Matilda added that whenever she could she not only tore the veil off, but threw it on the ground and jumped on it. Anselm eventually decided in her favour and the marriage went ahead. Edith-Matilda seems always to have been especially devoted to him, signing herself 'daughter of Anselm' in a charter and writing him loving letters while he was in political exile, but he never quite got over his suspicion of her.

Oxford, Bodleian Library, MS. Rawl. C. 149, 43r

That Edgar's long battle to achieve the Scottish throne had succeeded was due in no small measure to the support of his uncle and namesake, Edgar the Ætheling. In Germanic tradition men often had less troublesome relations with their sister's son than with their own son, since they could support their nephew's claims without damaging their own. Edgar the Ætheling led an adventurous life, with many political changes of fortune. He took part in the First Crusade, as well as numerous campaigns either with or against the Normans, and eventually retired to an estate in Hampshire, where he lived into his seventies.[31]

this manner), Henry I succeeded to the throne by immediately seizing the royal treasury and having himself crowned just three days after his brother's death. This left his elder brother, Robert Curthose, presented with a *fait accompli* when he arrived back in Normandy a month later from his participation in the First Crusade. Henry I was the fourth and last of William the Conqueror's sons, and the only one to have been born in England after the Conquest. At his coronation he issued a charter making in writing the same sorts of oaths as had always been made at English coronations, and promising to uphold the Anglo-Saxon laws observed in the time of Edward the Confessor over the laws of his father and brother.[32] The succession of Henry marked the possibility of a closer alliance between English and French factions at court.

Henry now arranged to marry Edith-Matilda, a plan in which he persisted against opposition from Archbishop Anselm who suspected that Edith-Matilda was a renegade nun. A few chroniclers say that Henry had long been in love with her, but the ancestry of her mother Margaret was certainly as important as any other consideration: as the *Anglo-Saxon Chronicle* says, she was 'of the rightful royal family of England'. The Norman nobles were certainly aware of this aspect of the alliance; according to William of Malmesbury they mocked Henry I for going native, calling the royal couple 'Godric and Godgifu', two particularly old-fashioned Anglo-Saxon names.[33]

In 1066 on his deathbed Edward the Confessor had made a prophecy about a green branch which would be split off from a tree and removed three furlongs away but later rejoined to it.[34] His words were recorded soon after the event by one of Queen Edith's chaplains. Archbishop Stigand had dismissed this as the ramblings of an ill man, but the prophecy was taken seriously in the twelfth century. Some people thought that the three furlongs were the three Anglo-Norman kings, and that the succession of a child of Henry I and Edith-Matilda would reunite the green branch to the tree by returning the throne of England to a descendant of the Anglo-Saxon line. In 1102 Edith-Matilda gave birth to her daughter Matilda, the future empress. In 1103 an heir was born, named William; he was known as the Ætheling, the ancient Anglo-Saxon title for a prince, like his mother's uncle Edgar the Ætheling. William Ætheling united the most resonant of Norman names with the most English of titles, and represented in his person the union of the two peoples.

It was probably at about this time, raised to the highest estate in England and the mother of two small children with important futures, that Edith-Matilda commissioned a *Life* of her own mother from Turgot, whose response was approving:

> *I congratulate you that, having been made queen of the Angles by the King of the Angels, you have desired not only to hear, but also to be able to inspect continuously written words about the life of your mother, the queen, who always aspired eagerly to reach the realm of the angels.*

Ealle he hı oððe wıð feo ʒe sealde· oððe on hıs aʒenre hand heold·
ꞇ to ʒafle ʒe sette· for þan þe he ælcer manner ʒe haðoder ꞇ læ
peder ynfenuma beon polde· ꞇ spa þ þæs dæʒes þe he ʒe feoll·
he heafde on hıs aʒenre hand þ arceb rıce on cantpar byrıʒ·
ꞇ þ bıscop rıce on pınceast· ꞇ þ on sear byrıʒ· ꞇ· xi· abb rıcer
ealle to ʒafle ʒe sette· And þeah· þe ıch ıs lænʒ ylde· eall
þe þe ʒode þæs lað· ꞇ wıð full mannan· eall þ þær ʒe punelıc
on þısan lande on hıs tyman· ꞇ for þı þe þær forneah ealne
hıs leode lað· ꞇ ʒode andsæte· spa spa hıs ænde ætypde· for
þan þe he on mıdde raridan hıs unrıhte buten be hreopsun
ʒe ꞇ ælcere dædbote ʒe þat· On þæne þunresdæʒ he pær of
slaʒen· ꞇ þær on morʒen be byrıʒed· ꞇ syðþan he be byrıʒed pær·
þa prıtan þe þa neh handa pæron· hır broðer heanrıʒ to cyn
ʒe ʒe curıan· ꞇ he þær rıhte þ bısc rıce on pınceast pıllme ʒıf
raride ʒeaf· ꞇ sıþþan to lundene for· ꞇ on þan sunnan dæʒe
þer æft to forıan þa peofode on pest mynstre ʒode ꞇ eallan
folce be het ealle þa unrıht to aleʒʒenne þe on hıs broðer
tıman pærıan· ꞇ þa betstan laʒe to healdene þe on æntʒes
cynʒes dæʒe to forıan hım stodan· And hıne syððan æft þa
se bıscop of lundene maurıci to cynrʒe ʒe halʒode· ꞇ hı ealle
on þeosan lande to abuʒan· ꞇ aðas sporıan· ꞇ hıs men purdon·
And se cynʒ sona æft þa be þære ræde þe hı abutan pærıan·
þon bıscop rannulf of dunholme let nıman· ꞇ ın to þa turıe
on lundene let ʒe brınʒon· ꞇ þær healdan· Ða to forıan sce
mıchahel mæssan cō se arcebıscop anseahm of cantpar byrı
hıder tolande· spa spa se cynʒ heanrıʒ be hıs yrena rædhe hı
æft sende· for þan þe he pær ut of hıs lande ʒe farıen· for
þan mycelan unrıhte þe se cynʒ pıllın hım dyde· And sıð
þan sona þer æft se cynʒ ʒe nā orahalde hı to pıfe malcol
mes cynʒes dohter of scotlande· ꞇ ora aıʒarıeta þære ʒoda

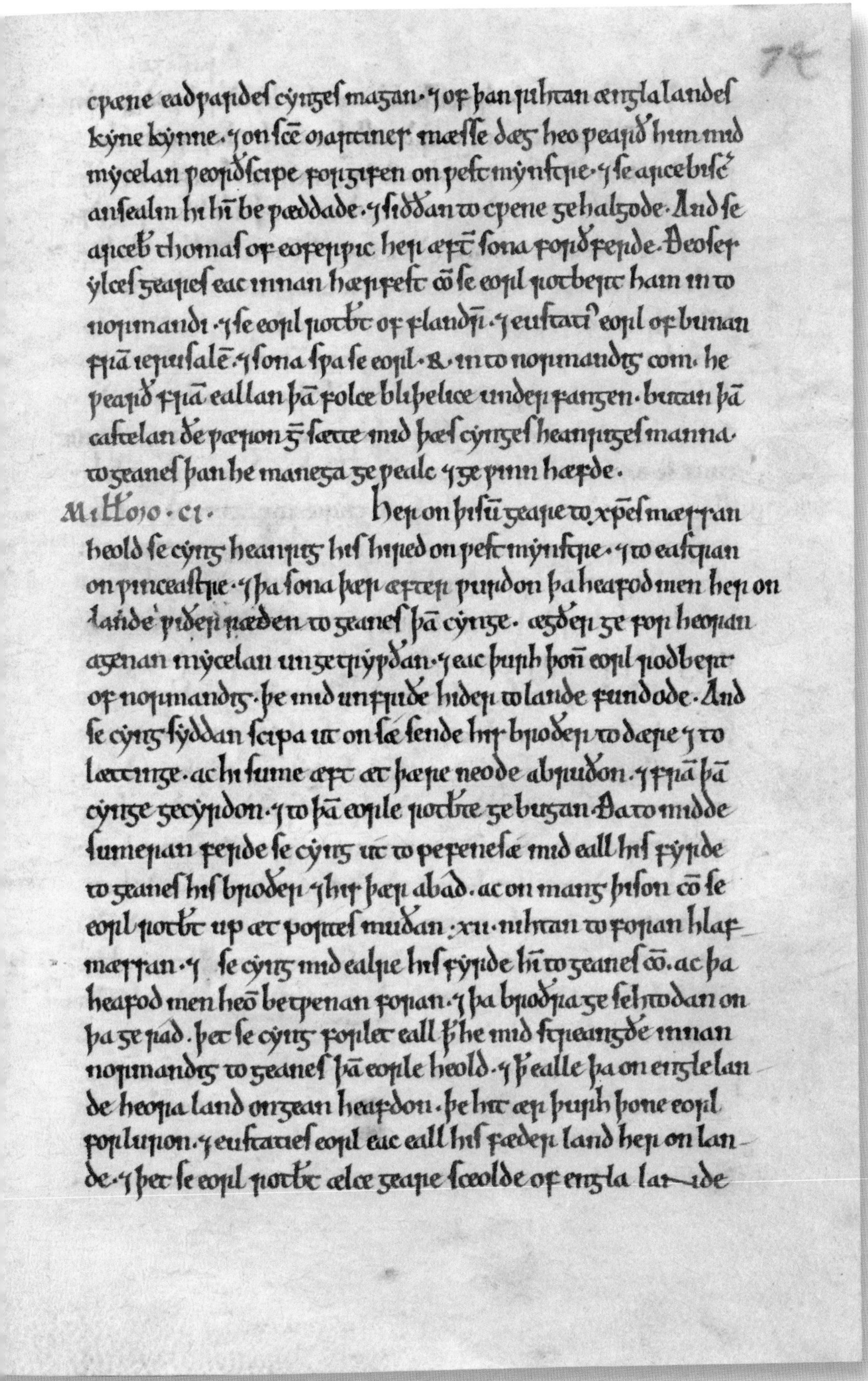

cpene eadpaþdef cynzef mazan · ⁊ of þan þihtan ænglalandef
kyne kynne · ⁊ on sͨē oſaꝛtinef mæsse dæz heo þeaꝛð him mid
mycelan þeoꝛðscipe foꝛzifen on pest mynstꝛe · ⁊ se aꝛcebisͨ
anfealm hi hi be pæddade · ⁊ siððan to cpene zehalzode · And se
aꝛceb̅ thomaf of eoꝛeꝛpic heꝛ æft sona foꝛð feꝛde · Þeofeꝛ
ylcef zeaꝛef eac innan hæꝛfest cō se eoꝛl ꝛoꝛbeꝛt ham in to
noꝛmandi · ⁊ se eoꝛl ꝛoꝛbt of flandꝛ̅ · ⁊ euftaci᷄ eoꝛl of bunan
fꝛā ieꝛufalē · ⁊ sona spa se eoꝛl · ꝛ · in to noꝛmandiz com · he
þeaꝛð fꝛā eallan þā folce bliþelice undeꝛ fanzen · butan þā
castelan ðe þeꝛon ᵹ sætte mid þef cynzef heaꝛꝛzef manna ·
to zeanef þan he maneza ze þeale · ⁊ ze pinn hæfde ·

Mℓℓoꝛo · ci ·   heꝛ on þisū zeaꝛe to xpͤf mæꝛꝛan
heold se cynz heaꝛꝛiz hif hiꝛed on pest mynstꝛe · ⁊ to eaftꝛan
on pinceaftꝛe · ⁊ þa sona heꝛ æfteꝛ puꝛdon þa heafod men heꝛ on
lande · pideꝛ pæden to zeanef þa cynze · æzðeꝛ ze foꝛ heoꝛan
azenan mycelan unzetꝛypdan · ⁊ eac buꝛh þon eoꝛl ꝛodbeꝛt
of noꝛmandiz · he mid unfꝛide hideꝛ to lande fundode · And
se cynz syððan scipa ut on se sende hiꝛ bꝛoðeꝛ to dæꝛe ⁊ to
lættinze · ac hi sume æft æt þeꝛe neode abꝛudon · ⁊ fꝛā þā
cynze zecyꝛdon · ⁊ to þā eoꝛle ꝛodbꝛe ze buzan · Ða to midde
sumeꝛan feꝛde se cynz ut to peꝛenesæ mid eall hif fyꝛde
to zeanef hif bꝛoðeꝛ · ⁊ hiꝛ þeꝛ þeꝛ abad · ac on manz þison cō se
eoꝛl ꝛodbt up æt poꝛtꝛes muðan · xii · nihtan to foꝛan hlaf
mæꝛꝛan · ⁊ se cynz mid ealꝛe hif fyꝛde hiꝛ to zeanef cō · ac þa
heafod men heo betꝛenan foꝛan · ⁊ þa bꝛoðꝛa ze sehtodan on
þa ze ꝛad · þet se cynz foꝛlet eall þ͞ he mid stꝛeanzðe innan
noꝛmandiz to zeanef þā eoꝛle heold · ⁊ þ͞ ealle þa on enzlelan
de heoꝛa land oꝛzean heafdon · he hit æꝛ buꝛh þone eoꝛl
foꝛluꝛon · ⁊ euftacief eoꝛl eac eall hif fædeꝛ land heꝛ on lan
de · ⁊ þet se eoꝛl ꝛodbt ælce zeaꝛe sceolde of enzla laꝛ̅de

FIGURE 56

'And then soon after [his coronation] the king took as his wife Maud, daughter of Malcolm king of Scotland and the good queen Margaret, kinswoman of King Edward, of the rightful royal family of England. And on St Martin's feast day she was given to him in Westminster with great honour, and archbishop Anselm married her to him and then consecrated her queen.'

Oxford, Bodleian Library, MS. Laud misc. 636, 73v-74r

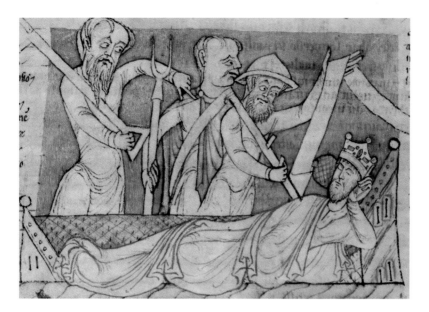

FIGURE 57
According to the *Chronicle of John of Worcester* Henry I had a dream in which the three estates, the peasants, the nobles, and the ecclesiastics, visited him in turn to complain about excessive taxes: this image shows the peasants menacing the king with pitchforks and scythes.[16] This part of this manuscript was probably written out by John of Worcester himself. Edith-Matilda was credited with helping to rein in her husband's rapacity.

Oxford, Corpus Christi College, MS. 157, p. 382

It seems likely that Edith-Matilda understood the *Life's* didactic purpose better than many modern scholars. Her younger brother David, later king of Scotland, told how during his youth at the Anglo-Norman court Edith-Matilda once summoned him from a feast. He found her in her chamber surrounded by lepers, devotedly washing and kissing their feet:[35]

> *'What are you doing, my lady?' he asked. 'Surely if the king knew about this he would never deign to kiss with his lips your mouth which has been polluted by the sores of lepers' feet.' Then she said, amused, 'Do you not know that the lips of the eternal king are preferable to those of a king who will die?'*

She urged David to join her; but, to his later shame, he returned laughing to the feast. This took place in 1105; quite possibly Edith-Matilda had been inspired by Turgot's recently-completed *Life* of her mother.

She was famous for many of the same virtues as her mother, in particular for a very practical kind of piety. She set up a leper house at St Giles-in-the-Fields, a little removed from the centre of London for sanitary reasons, and in Aldgate she founded a house of Augustinian canons to work among the poor. (She dedicated it to the Holy Trinity, echoing her mother's devotion.) At Queenhithe she built a bathhouse, including London's first recorded public lavatory. She seems to have been a particular benefactor to London, perhaps because of the city's political importance, but she also gave lands and other gifts to monasteries throughout England, including her *alma mater*, Wilton Abbey. The land she gave to Tynemouth monastery for the sake of her father's soul is particularly interesting, because it had once belonged to Archil Tyrel, the man popularly credited with killing Malcolm in an ambush. Edith-Matilda acted as regent for Henry I on occasion, during his absence

FIGURE 58

By her death in 1118 Edith-Matilda was
spared knowledge of the disaster that
befell her family in 1120. The Anglo-
Norman court was returning from a visit
to Normandy; King Henry sailed first
and on the next day his son and heir, as
well as many of the Anglo-Norman
nobility, followed in the White Ship, a
brand new vessel. There was a celebratory
atmosphere on board and the crew and
passengers were dangerously drunk. The
ship struck a rock outside Barfleur and
sank with only one survivor, a butcher
from Rouen. According to legend
William was about to escape in a small
boat when he heard his half-sister crying
out from the wreck, and went back to get
her; he was never seen again. According
to the *Anglo-Saxon Chronicle*, it was a
double grief to the loved ones of the
lost, that they died so suddenly and that
most of their bodies were never
recovered. After the death of his heir
King Henry is said never to have smiled
again. He remarried, but did not have
another legitimate son.

Oxford, Corpus Christi College, MS. 157, p. 383

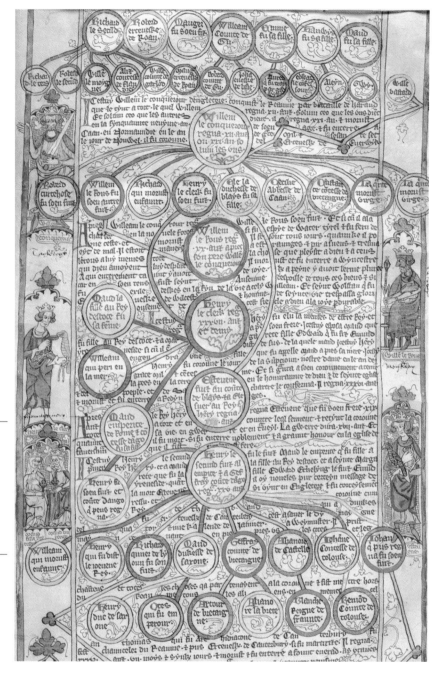

FIGURE 59

In this genealogical roll Matilda, daughter of Malcolm and Margaret, sits talking with her daughter, Matilda the Empress. Both carry sceptres, or possibly palms; this may be intended to hint at their connection with the queen of heaven, Mary, who is often portrayed carrying a similar object. The younger Matilda left England at the age of eight to be brought up as the affianced spouse of the King of the Romans, later Emperor Henry V; she was married just before she turned twelve. At fifteen she was crowned Empress in Rome, though not by the Pope himself, but she was left a childless widow at the age of twenty-three. She returned to England and was formally made her father's heir. She then married Geoffrey Plantagenet, who succeeded to the county of Anjou when his father abdicated it to become King of Jerusalem by marriage to the redoubtable queen Melisende. But on Henry I's death in 1135, his nephew Stephen (whose wife was, like the empress, a grand-daughter of St Margaret) contested the succession, and 'The Anarchy' followed, when 'people said openly that Christ and his angels slept'.[57]

Oxford, Bodleian Library, MS. Ashmole Rolls 38, sheet 5

across the sea, and was credited with persuading him to amend bad laws or uphold old good ones. She also supported the arts, commissioning historical works and poetry from Latin writers. It was probably at her instigation that William of Malmesbury wrote his most famous work, the *Gesta regum Anglorum*, or 'Deeds of the English Kings'.

Edith-Matilda died on 1 May 1118, aged only thirty-eight. She was widely seen as a good influence on her somewhat difficult husband, encouraging charity and lawfulness, and in this she fully lived up to her mother's example. In fact, there were reports of miracles at her tomb in Westminster Abbey, and if her son William had succeeded after Henry I's death she would probably have been venerated as a saint.

Margaret's other daughter, Mary, was married by Henry I to Count Eustace of Boulogne; her daughter Matilda married Stephen, nephew of Henry I, who contested the Empress' right to the throne, causing the Anarchy.

David I

The two youngest sons of Margaret and Malcolm were Alexander and David. At the death of Edgar without sons in early 1107 the two brothers became heirs of Scotland. David inherited control over some of the southernmost part of the kingdom, but Alexander succeeded to the kingship. He had married one of Henry I's illegitimate daughters, Sybilla; but they had no children and, according to William of Malmesbury:

> when she died he did not much lament her loss, because there was, they say, some defect about the lady, either in correctness of manners or in elegance of person.[38]

Alexander had been the only layman present at the opening of the tomb of St Cuthbert in 1104, and had given a large donation to pay for the new shrine. He had a reputation for piety, and like his sister he sponsored poets.

David was probably only about nine years old when his parents died, and he seems to have taken refuge in Wessex with his sisters; he was a great favourite of Edith-Matilda, and also of her husband Henry I. Around 1113 Henry gave David the hand in marriage of one of England's richest heiresses, Matilda of Huntingdon. She was the daughter of William the Conqueror's much-loved niece Judith and of Earl Waltheof, son of Siward of Northumbria. Waltheof had been executed by William the Conqueror for his part in an English rebellion to put David's uncle Edgar the Ætheling on the throne, and was revered as a saint in some East Anglian

Henry I had a very large number of illegitimate children, over twenty recorded to history; he made great use of the daughters in marriage alliances, and of the sons as supporters of his rule who could not threaten him or his heirs by their own claim to the throne. According to William of Malmesbury, the fornication Henry indulged in as a youth was allowable because he did not do it for pleasure, but out of foresight to engender bastards for political purposes: 'thus he was the master of his libido, not its servant'.[39] He did not marry until he was king, perhaps in order that his heirs would have the extra distinction of being 'born in the purple', after their father's coronation, just as Henry had been himself. In this he miscalculated; he survived his only legitimate son, and his death in 1135 plunged the kingdom into nearly twenty years of anarchy.

and West-Saxon areas. Matilda was Waltheof's heiress, and held vast estates in the east of England in her own right. (She had been married previously but was now widowed.) She would have been about forty years old at this time, and David probably not yet thirty.

At the death of King Alexander in 1124 after a seventeen-year rule, David succeeded to the throne of Scotland. He was now aged about forty and according to William of Malmesbury, he had spent so much time at the English court that he had: 'rubbed off all the rust of Scottish barbarism'. [40] The influence of his mother Margaret and of his sister Edith-Matilda is clearly evident in the many grants he made to religious houses. He is often referred to as St David; James I (1406–37), reviewing his ancestor's generosity with royal property, famously called him 'a sair sanct to the croun'. David was very much influenced by his years at the Anglo-Norman court, and his continued links with it after his succession, when he retained his lands in the east of England. He introduced the first royal coinage to Scotland, based on Anglo-Norman models which in their turn were based on the sophisticated Anglo-Saxon coinage system. He supported his niece Matilda during the anarchy, invading Northumbria in her cause; although it must be said that medieval Scottish kings were always glad of a reason to raid Northumbria, David I imposed some peace and stability in the north at a time when it was desperately lacking in the south. He was celebrated as a great lawgiver, and is sometimes called Scotland's greatest king. By David's death in 1153 he had achieved such stability that his grandson Malcolm IV, aged only twelve, was able to succeed him peacefully, in contrast to the dynastic struggles which had preceded the succession of David's father Malcolm III nearly a century earlier.

MIRACLES

Margaret was certainly already viewed as a saint in the twelfth century. Symeon of Durham, writing in the first quarter of the twelfth century, called her the saintly queen, and later in the same century Reginald of Durham related how a procession of her relics was held at Dunfermline on the date of her death, attended by a large number of people, both men and women.[42] Aelred of Rievaulx described Margaret to her great-grandson Henry II as 'a most saintly woman'.[43] Roger of Hoveden, writing only a few years after the event, related how in 1199 the king of

> David I's closeness to his sister Edith-Matilda can be seen in a grant he made to her burial place, Westminster Abbey, of thirty shillings a year; four shillings were to be distributed as charity on each of his parents' death days, and the remaining twenty-two were for Edith-Matilda's anniversary. Of the last, three shillings were to be spent on four candles (two for the eve and two for the day), ten on wine, six on alms, and three shillings on superior wine at the feast.[41]

FIGURE 60
The Norman nave at Dunfermline Abbey
Margaret and Malcolm were married at Dunfermline, and Margaret later founded a Benedictine abbey there, with the help of Lanfranc, the archbishop of Canterbury. Her son David I continued her work. When Malcolm and Margaret died within days of each other they were buried together in the abbey.

Scotland, William the Lion, spent the night in vigil at St Margaret's tomb while on the verge of invading England.[44] His great-grandmother appeared to him in a vision, and on her sensible advice he abandoned the proposed invasion. (Unhappily for Scotland, he resumed his plans later.)

In 1249 or 1250 Margaret was officially canonized by Pope Innocent IV. She is thus the only officially canonized Scottish saint, as opposed to saints who were simply accorded that title through popular devotion. (One might, however, also count St William of Perth, who was murdered in around 1201 at Rochester by a foundling he had taken in, although his veneration does not seem to have spread outside Kent.) On 19 June 1251 Margaret's remains were translated from her grave at Dunfermline Abbey into a shrine of silver and precious stones which was placed under the high altar. According to medieval stories of the translation, Margaret's bones were too heavy to lift until someone hit upon the idea of transporting her husband Malcolm's remains too, whereupon Margaret showed her consent by becoming light enough to be moved.

A collection of the miracles that happened through Margaret's intercession was made in the middle of the thirteenth century, probably as part of the drive to have her canonized.[45] It shows that people sought her help from England as well as Scotland; frequently she appeared to them in visions, wearing shining or colourful dress. She often seems to have helped people possessed by devils: she plucked enchanted apples from throats, fought off demonic shaggy dogs, and on two separate occasions she cured people by making them vomit up a huge quantity of lizards. In 1263 she appeared to a knight just before an important battle with a Norwegian invasion fleet. She was mounted on a horse, and riding after her were Malcolm and their sons Edgar, Alexander, and David. She explained to the knight that she was leading them to the defence of the kingdom:

For I have accepted this kingdom from God and it is entrusted to me and my heirs forever.

Margaret was venerated throughout the Middle Ages; often, we might suspect, for political reasons. In 1303 Edward I of England, 'the hammer of the Scots', gave jewels at her shrine, and his queen Marguerite of France also made a donation later in the same year. In 1315 Robert the Bruce, who had wrested control of Scotland back from the English, also gave gifts to St Margaret. In the fourteenth century her cult had spread sufficiently into England that there were minor relics of Margaret at Coldingham, Durham, Worcester, Windsor, and in a portable reliquary belonging to Edward III.

In the fourteenth century a short version of Margaret's *life*, emphasizing her royal ancestry, was made as part of a collection of saints' 'Lives' by a vicar called John of Tynemouth.[46] He added to the end David's story of Edith-Matilda washing lepers' feet. In the only surviving manuscript of this collection of lives, many of the lower margins contain added prayers to the

FIGURE 61

St Margaret of Antioch was a very popular saint in the Middle Ages, and Margaret of Scotland was probably named after her. According to her legend, she was in prison during the persecution of Diocletian when she saw a vision of a terrible dragon which swallowed her whole. She did not fear, however, but made the sign of a Cross, whereupon she burst out of its stomach unharmed. She was consequently the patron saint of childbirth, among other things. Two versions of her *Life* survive in Old English. This picture from a Book of Hours shows her emerging from the dragon's stomach before he has even quite finished swallowing the train of her dress. It seems that pregnant women also turned to Margaret of Scotland, probably because of her name; her sark, or under shirt, was brought to aid Queens of Scotland in childbirth, and at the Reformation her Cross at Durham was said to be 'good for those lying in'.

Oxford, Bodleian Library, MS. Lat. liturg. g. 5, p. 98

saints whose lives are found in the main text; but underneath the 'Life of Margaret' instead there is a diagram of her descendants, showing how much her family connections were still valued at this date.

AFTER THE REFORMATION
Margaret's tomb

Dunfermline was destroyed in 1560, and St Margaret's shrine was plundered. However, a silver and ebony reliquary, set with precious stones and pearls, containing Margaret's head and long auburn hair, was hidden from the reformers in the possession of the Laird of Dury, a former monk of Dunfermline. Mary Queen of Scots had this relic of Margaret brought to Edinburgh Castle while she was there awaiting the birth of her son, the future James I and VI, in the spring of 1566. In 1597 it was taken to Belgium by a Jesuit priest, John Robie. It was displayed at Antwerp before being taken to the Scottish College at Douay, a place where Catholic exiles could study for the priesthood before returning to their native land. A plenary indulgence was granted by Pope Innocent X to anyone who prayed before it. The relic is last recorded there in 1785; it was probably destroyed in the chaos of the French Revolution.

The rest of Margaret's relics were sent to Philip II of Spain, with the remains of Malcolm, at his request in 1563. He placed them in two urns in a chapel in the Escorial. In 1863 Bishop James Gillies obtained a relic of Margaret from this source by petitioning Pope Pius IX.

Margaret's Gospel-book

The first definite owner we know of Margaret's Gospels after the Reformation is John Stow, who wrote his name in his distinctive hand on the back of the last leaf of the book. John Stow (1524/5–1605) was a sixteenth-century antiquary who amassed vast quantities of material from medieval chronicles, and collected manuscripts and printed books. Although Stow does not seem to have travelled much, he acquired or borrowed books from many places.

By the end of the sixteenth century the book had passed into the hands of Lord William Howard (1563–1640), the third son of Thomas Howard, fourth duke of Norfolk. Lord William Howard had his seat at Naworth in Cumbria. He was a very powerful man on the English–Scottish borders, famous for his tough attitude to raiders — Walter Scott immortalized him as 'Belted Will' in *The Lay of the Last Minstrel*. Howard had the manuscript rebound; he is unlikely to have removed a valuable binding from the book to replace it with a plain one, so we can deduce that the book had lost its treasure binding by this stage.

Sir Walter Scott, The Lay of the Last Minstrel, *canto 5, stanza 16:*

> *When for the lists they sought the plain,*
> *The stately Ladye's silken rein*
> > *Did noble Howard hold;*
> *Unarmed by her side he walk'd,*
> *And much, in courteous phrase, they talk'd*
> > *Of feats of arms of old.*
> *Costly his garb; his Flemish ruff*
> *Fell o'er his doublet, shap'd of buff,*
> > *With satin slash'd and lin'd;*
> *Tawny his boot, and gold his spur,*
> *His cloak was all of Poland fur,*
> > *His hose with silver twin'd;*
> *His Bilboa blade, by Marchmen felt,*
> *Hung in a broad and studded belt;*
> *Hence, in rude phrase, the Borderers still*
> *Call'd noble Howard, Belted Will.*

'The Norman Yoke' and the Perfect Princess

In the seventeenth century England was shaken by the Civil War, and Parliament forces successfully deposed King Charles I. At this period several radical groups of political activists arose, including the Levellers, who gained that name from their opponents' accusation that they wanted all people to be equal, and the Diggers, who argued that land should be owned and cultivated in common. The idea arose of the 'Norman Yoke'; it was held that the current ruling classes were all descended from foreign invaders who had quashed the Anglo-Saxon golden age as represented by the reigns of Alfred the Great and Edward the Confessor. One of the Diggers, Gerrard Winstanley, wrote in 1649, the year that Charles I was executed:[47]

> *Seeing the common people of England by joynt consent of person and purse have caste out Charles our Norman oppressour, wee have by this victory recovered ourselves from under his Norman yoake.*

In 1660 an edition of Turgot's *Life of Margaret* was printed in France, dedicated to the then-exiled Charles II, and an English translation was published in 1661, just after the Restoration.[48] The political purpose of this work is made very clear in the introduction: it is to counter the idea promulgated by the 'phanatiques' that the Stuarts represent the Norman line; Charles II is not only descended from the ancient Anglo-Saxon kings, but this descent is through Margaret, whose goodness justifies the idea of Divine Right.

From this time onwards Margaret was increasingly used by the Stuart line to add legitimacy to their cause. The Catholic James II was forced to abdicate the throne in the Glorious Revolution of 1688, in favour of his daughter Mary's husband William of Orange, the Protestant Defender. In 1693 Pope Innocent XII instituted a celebration of St Margaret's Day throughout the Catholic world on 10 June; in his decree he explicitly stated that this was in compliment to James II's infant son whose birthday this was. (The date of 10 June had first been set as Margaret's feast in 1673 but then changed to 8 July in 1678: there is no obvious reason for the choice of either of these dates.) After James II's death his son was known as 'The Old Pretender' in England but as James III in Catholic Europe. In 1717, soon after James's failed landing in Scotland and the French king's abandonment of his claims, Pope Clement XI celebrated the Mass of St Margaret with James in St Peter's as a gesture of support for James's claim to the British throne.

Catherine Fane

In the early eighteenth century St Margaret's Gospel-book was owned by a certain Fane Edge, vicar of Nedging in Suffolk; he bequeathed it to the parish library of nearby Brent Eleigh.

FIGURE 62
Margaret and Malcolm in a heraldic manuscript of the sixteenth century. The inclusion of Margaret as well as Malcolm shows that her ancestry continued to be important even centuries after her death. She wears the arms of Edward the Confessor on her skirt.
Oxford, Bodleian Library, MS. Wood C. 9, 4r

King Malcolm Cann more marijt
Saint Margaret of Dunfermling
scho bar to him ane sone
callit Edward quhilk succedit
to ye trone þ deit without
successioun gottin of his body
and efter succedit to him
king robert bruce nerrest
to ye said Edward of blude

THE
IDÆA
OF A
PERFECT
PRINCESSE,
IN
The life of St. *Margaret* Queen of
SCOTLAND.

With Elogiums on her Children, *David,*
and *Mathilda* Queen of *England.*

Written Originally in French, and now Englished.

WHEREUNTO

Is annexed a Postscript, clearly proving, against the
false pretences of the *Phanaticks,* his Majesties just
right and Title to the Crown of *England,* and to his
other Dominions, before the Conquest.

Never before published.

Paris Anno 1661.

IOHN STOW. HISTORIAN & ANTIQUARY.
(*From His Monument in the Church of St Andrew, Undershaft.*)

John Stow, who was bred a Taylor, quitted his Occupation, to pursue his beloved study of the History & Antiquities of England, to which he had an invincible propensity. He was not only indefatigable in searching for ancient Authors & MSS of all kinds relating to English History, but was also at the pains of transcribing many things with his own hand, as his studies & Collections engrossed his whole attention, he, in a few years found himself in embarrassed circumstances, & was under a necessity of returning to his trade, but was enabled by the generosity of Arch. Bishop Parker to resume his Studies, his principal Works, are his Survey of London: a Book deservedly esteemed, his additions to Hollensheds Chronicle, and his Annals, the folio Volume, commonly called Stows Chronicle, was compiled from his papers after his decease, by E. Howes, our Author Stow, had a principal hand in two improved editions of Chaucers works, published in this reign Ob. 5. April 1605, Æ. 80 see Grangier P. 269, & Pennants London P. 397.

Publish'd May 10.1792 by N. Smith, N.º 18. G.t Mays Buildings S.t Martins Lane.

But it was not the only manuscript he gave them; a group of eight manuscripts came to the library this way. At least four of these, including St Margaret's Gospel-book, had been owned by Lord William Howard, and another by his aunt, the countess of Westmorland. Most of William Howard's books went to his nephew, Thomas Howard earl of Arundel, and thence into the Arundel collection, most of which is now in the British Library; but at least one of Fane Edge's small group of books was owned by William Howard's son, which might explain why they took a different path.

Fane Edge had inherited the manuscript from his mother, Catherine Fane, who was the daughter of Rev. William Fane, the sixth son of Francis Fane, first Earl of Westmorland in the second creation. The original creation of the Earldom of Westmorland (to which William Howard's aunt Jane had belonged by marriage) had died out after a number of its members were involved in Catholic conspiracies, and seems to have had only a tangential connection with the second creation. Catherine's mother was a certain Frances Rodney, of the Rodney family

of Somerset, which apparently had some connection with the Howard family. The Howard family extended its already large influence by marrying into many families — William Howard's great-grandfather, the third Duke of Norfolk, had even managed to marry two of his nieces to Henry VIII, with unhappy results.

Catherine Fane also had Howard connections on her father's side, since her grandmother, wife of Francis Fane, was Mary Mildmay. Mary was the granddaughter and heiress of Sir Walter Mildmay, founder of Emmanuel College, Cambridge, and it was through her that the Fanes had inherited their country seat at Apethorpe. Walter Mildmay seems to have been a friend of William Howard's father Phillip, and was remembered in his will — though they were on opposite sides of political issues of the day, and Elizabeth I used Mildmay in her dealings with Mary Queen of Scots. There are rather too many possibilities as to how St Margaret's Gospel-book could have entered the hands of Catherine Fane in the seventeenth century, and at present none can be settled on as more likely than any other.

The Bodleian Library and Lucy Hill

The Bodleian Library acquired Margaret's Gospel-book at auction in 1887, for only six pounds, a small sum even then. Its connection with St Margaret was long forgotten, and furthermore the Sotheby's sale catalogue had erroneously dated it to the fourteenth century. In the same year Lucy Hill, daughter of George Birkbeck Hill, read the poem written in the front of the manuscript and was reminded of the episode in the *Life of St Margaret*; she was able to identify the manuscript as Margaret's Gospel-book for the first time in centuries.

FIGURE 65
The little Suffolk village of Brent Eleigh was home to Margaret's Gospels for over a century and a half. The library set up here by Henry Colman *circa* 1700 had only one manuscript until Fane Edge bequeathed a further eight. When some whitewash was removed from the interior of the church in 1960, this fourteenth-century altarpiece was uncovered.
Altarpiece at St Mary's, Brent Eleigh

One of Fane Edge's books had been owned by William Howard's aunt, the countess of Westmorland; this is a little fifteenth-century prayerbook with the name of Mary Queen of Scots written in a margin. Jane Neville, Countess of Westmorland, foolishly urged her husband into involvement in a plot to free Mary Queen of Scots from her English captivity and marry her to Thomas Howard, Duke of Norfolk, Jane's brother. Unsurprisingly Elizabeth I disapproved of and successfully quashed this plan, and Jane was left a grass widow after her husband's flight to the Spanish Netherlands.

FIGURE 66 *above*

We do not know how Margaret's Gospels got from Lord William Howard (d. 1640), to Catherine Fane, who was married half a century later. We know that the Fane family inherited some books (as well as their family seat) from the Mildmay family, and there is some link between William Howard's father and Walter Mildmay. Grace Mildmay, Catherine Fane's great-grandmother and Walter Mildmay's daughter-in-law, wrote one of the earliest surviving English autobiographies by a woman. She was renowned for her practical piety and her charity was remembered long after her death; it would be very fitting if she had owned St Margaret's Gospel-book, but this is only one of several possibilities. This picture of Grace Mildmay, above, now destroyed, shows her in old age.

Grace Mildmay, from a now-lost portrait

FIGURE 67 *above*

It was Lucy Hill, later Lucy Hill Crump, who recognized that the Bodleian's acquisition had once belonged to St Margaret of Scotland. She was only twenty-two at the time. She seems to have had a particular interest in the formidable religious women of history; she wrote several books in later life including a translation of the memoirs Charlotte Arbaleste de Mornay, an important Huguenot woman.

Lucy Hill in 1887, by Arthur Hughes

Conclusion

The happy survival of St Margaret's Gospel-book gives us a small window into the life and mind of an eleventh-century queen. From this personal little book of only thirty-eight leaves we can learn much about Margaret, a fascinating and unusual woman whose significance as a historical figure of reconciliation lasted long into the modern age. But the manuscript is also attractive and interesting in its own right, with its simple but effective design and beautiful illumination.

The Family Tree of St Margaret

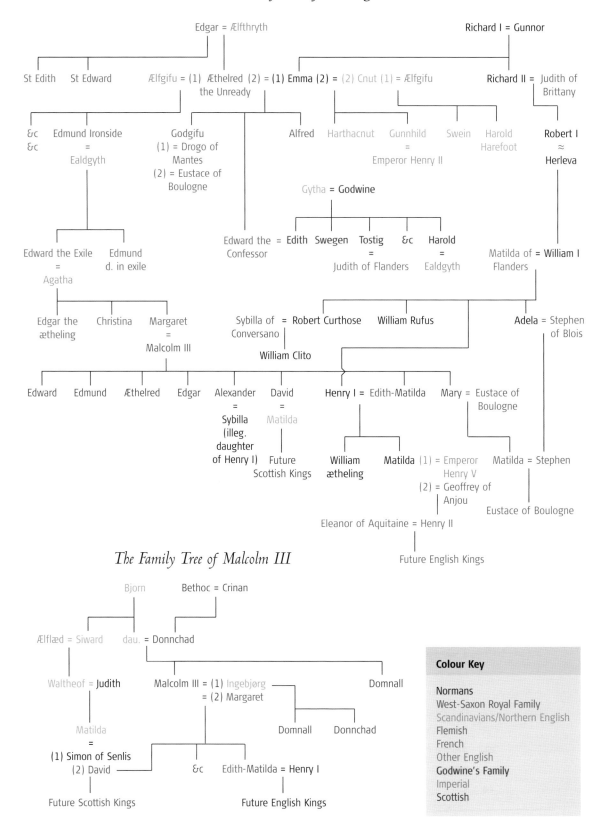

Edgar = Ælfthryth

Richard I = Gunnor

St Edith   St Edward   Ælfgifu = (1) Æthelred (2) = (1) Emma (2) = (2) Cnut (1) = Ælfgifu   Richard II = Judith of
                                   the Unready   Brittany

&c   Edmund Ironside   Godgifu   Alfred   Harthacnut   Gunnhild   Swein   Harold   Robert I
&c   =   (1) = Drogo of   =   Harefoot   ≈
         Ealdgyth   Mantes   Emperor Henry II   Herleva
                         (2) = Eustace of
                         Boulogne

                                    Gytha = Godwine

                         Edward the = Edith Swegen Tostig   &c   Harold
                         Confessor   =   =
                                         Judith of Flanders Ealdgyth

Edward the Exile   Edmund   Matilda of = William I
        =   d. in exile   Flanders
     Agatha

Edgar the   Christina   Margaret   Sybilla of = Robert Curthose   William Rufus   Adela = Stephen
ætheling   =   Conversano   of Blois
                         Malcolm III   William Clito

Edward Edmund Æthelred Edgar Alexander David   Henry I = Edith-Matilda   Mary = Eustace of
                                      =   =   Boulogne
                                   Sybilla   Matilda
                                   (illeg.
                                   daughter   Future   William   Matilda (1) = Emperor   Matilda = Stephen
                                   of Henry I) Scottish   ætheling   Henry V
                                              Kings   (2) = Geoffrey of   Eustace of Boulogne
                                                                            Anjou
                                                          Eleanor of Aquitaine = Henry II

                                                                    Future English Kings

The Family Tree of Malcolm III

Bjorn   Bethoc = Crinan

Ælflæd = Siward   dau. = Donnchad

Waltheof = Judith   Malcolm III = (1) Ingebjørg   Domnall
                                 = (2) Margaret
    Matilda   Domnall Donnchad
       =
(1) Simon of Senlis
(2) David   &c   Edith-Matilda = Henry I

Future Scottish Kings   Future English Kings

Colour Key

Normans
West-Saxon Royal Family
Scandinavians/Northern English
Flemish
French
Other English
Godwine's Family
Imperial
Scottish

Notes

1. This excerpt is from the *Life of St Margaret*, supposedly by Turgot, printed in *Acta Sanctorum Junius II*, cols. 0320A–0340E. For a translation see Huneycutt, *Matilda*, pp. 161–78.

2. This poem, found on 2r of the manuscript, has been edited and translated by Gameson, 'The Gospels of Margaret of Scotland', pp. 165–6.

3. Symeon of Durham, *Historia Dunelmensis Ecclesiae*, II.11–13; for a translation see Brown, *The Lindisfarne Gospels*, pp. 110–11.

4. Bray, *A list of motifs in the lives of the early Irish saints*.

5. On Alfred see Keynes and Lapidge, *Alfred the Great*.

6. See 'Cerdic' in *The Blackwell Encyclopedia of Anglo-Saxon England*, p. 93.

7. See Keynes, facs. edn., *The Liber Vitae of the New Minster*.

8. See Barlow, ed. and trans., *The Life of King Edward*.

9. See Gwara and Porter, ed. and trans., *Anglo-Saxon Conversations*, colloquy XXIV, pp. 130–7.

10. Rackham *et al.*, ed. and trans., *Pliny's Natural History*, XIII:XXI, vol. IV, pp. 138–41.

11. For the *Anglo-Saxon Chronicle* see the edition by Plummer and the translation by Swanton, both in the further reading section.

12. Thompson, facs. edn., *Liber Vitae Ecclesiae Dunelmensis*, 48v.

13. Clover and Gibson, ed. and trans., *The Letters of Lanfranc*, no. 50, pp. 160–3.

14. The text of the letter is in Migne, ed., *Patrologia Latina* 163, col. 765.

15. See *Acta Sanctorum Februarius I*, cols. 0289B–0294E.

16. Printed in *Acta Sanctorum Junius II*, cols. 0320A–0340E, translated by Huneycutt, *Matilda*, pp. 161–78.

17. On St Edith see Hollis *et al.*, *Writing the Wilton Women*.

18. From the 'Life of King Edward' as transmitted by Richard of Chichester; see Barlow, ed. and trans., *The Life of King Edward*, p. 22.

19. Bede's *Historia Ecclesiastica*, III.3, Colgrave and Mynors, ed. and trans., *Bede's Ecclesiastical History*, pp. 218–21.

20. See Bede's *De temporum ratione*, ch. 6, Wallis, trans., *Bede: The Reckoning of Time*, pp. 24–8.

21. *Elene* has been edited by Krapp, *The Vercelli Book*, pp. 66–102, and translated by Bradley, *Anglo-Saxon Poetry*, pp. 164–97.

22. For Anglo-Saxon Gospel pericopes see Lenker, *Die Westsächsische Evangelienversion*.

23. *Andreas* has been edited by Krapp, *The Vercelli Book*, pp. 30–51, and translated by Bradley, *Anglo-Saxon Poetry*, pp. 110–153.

24. On Judith's books see McGurk and Rosenthal, 'The Anglo-Saxon Gospelbooks of Judith'.

25. See Ellis and Elsworth, *The Book of Deer*.

26. Edinburgh, University Library, MS. 56; Finlayson, facs. edn., *Celtic Psalter*.

27. Günzel, ed., *Ælfwine's Prayerbook*.

28. Reginald of Durham, *Libellus*, in Raine, ed., *Reginaldi Monachi*, ch. 98.

29. Fowler, *Extracts from the Account Rolls of Durham*, pp. 425–39.

30. Obit added to the calendar in Rome, Bibliotheca Apostolica Vaticana, MS. Reg. lat. 12, 'The Bury Psalter'.

31. Hooper, 'Edgar the Ætheling'.

32. Translated by Douglas and Greenaway in *English Historical Documents II*, pp. 432–4.

33. Mynors *et al.*, ed. and trans., *William of Malmesbury, Gesta regum Anglorum*, V.394, pp. 716–17.

34. See Barlow, ed. and trans, *The Life of King Edward*, pp. 75–8.

35. In Aelred of Rievaulx's *Genealogia regum Anglorum*, ed. Migne, in *Patrologia Latina*, vol. 195 col. 736.

36. McGurk, ed. and trans., *The Chronicle of John of Worcester*, year 1131, pp. 198–203.

37. *The Anglo-Saxon Chronicle*, E-version, for the year 1137; edited by Plummer, *Two of the Saxon Chronicles*; translated by Swanton, *The Anglo-Saxon Chronicle*.

38. Mynors *et al.*, ed. and trans. *Gesta regum Anglorum*, V.400, pp. 724–7.

39. Mynors *et al.*, ed. and trans. *Gesta regum Anglorum*, V.412, pp. 744–7.

40. Mynors *et al.*, ed. and trans. *Gesta regum Anglorum*, V.400, pp. 724–7.

41. Barrow, ed., *The Charters of King David I*, no. 13, p. 58.

42. Symeon of Durham's *Historia Regum* has been edited by Arnold, *Symeonis monachi opera omnia*, and translated by Stephenson, *Simeon of Durham*. Reginald of Durham's *Libellus* has been edited by Raine, *Reginaldi monachi*; ch. 98 contains the procession.

43. In his *Genealogia regum Anglorum*, ed. Migne, in *Patrologia Latina* 195, col. 716.

44. Stubbs, ed., *Chronica Magistri Rogeri de Houedene*, vol. IV p. 100.

45. Bartlett, ed. and trans., *The Miracles of Saint Æbbe*.

46. This survives as London, British Library, MS. Cotton Tiberius E. I.

47. Winstanley, *An Appeal to the House of Commons*, p. 7.

48. Leslie, *The idaea of a perfect princesse*; first published in French as *L'Idée d'une reine parfaite en la vie de S. Marguerite reine d'Escosse, avec les Eloges de ses enfans Dauid & Matilde* (Douay, 1660).

List of illustrations

Illustrations appear by kind permission and are copyright of the following bodies:

Nos. 1, 3, 6, 8, 12–17, 19–23, 25, 28, 30–32, 41–5, 47, 49, 51, 54–6, 59, 61–2, 64: Bodleian Library, University of Oxford

Nos. 2, 53, 60: Crown Copyright, Historic Scotland Images

Nos. 4, 38, 46, 48: the Master and Fellows of University College, Oxford

Nos. 5, 10: The Ashmolean Museum, Oxford

Nos. 7, 57–8: The Master and Fellows of Corpus Christi College, Oxford

Nos. 9, 37, 39: The British Library

No. 11: Timothy Rushforth

Nos. 18, 24, 26: The Master and Fellows of Pembroke College, Cambridge

Nos. 27, 34–6: The Master and Fellows of Corpus Christi College, Cambridge

No. 29: Bibliothèque municipale, Rouen

Nos. 33, 50: Pierpont Morgan Library, New York

No. 40: Dean and Chapter of Salisbury Cathedral

No. 52: Dean and Chapter of Durham Cathedral

Nos. 63, 66: National Portrait Gallery

No. 65: Anne Marshall, www.paintedchurch.org

No. 67: Sotheby's

Further Reading

W. Forbes-Leith, facs. edn., *The Gospel Book of St Margaret* (Edinburgh, 1896)

R. Gameson, 'The Gospels of Margaret of Scotland and the Literacy of an Eleventh-Century Queen', in *Women and the Book: Assessing the Visual Evidence*, ed. L. Smith and J. H. M. Taylor (London, 1997), pp. 149–71.

Medieval manuscripts

M. Brown and P. Lovett, *The Historical Source Book for Scribes* (London, 1999).

M. Brown, *A Guide to Western Historical Scripts from Antiquity to 1600* (London, 1990).

C. de Hamel, *A History of Medieval Manuscripts* (Oxford, 1985)

P. Lovett *et al.*, *The British Library Companion to Calligraphy, Illumination and Heraldry* (London, 2000).

M. Brown, *The Lindisfarne Gospels: Society, Spirituality and the Scribe* (London, 2003).

P. B. Ellis and R. Elsworth, *The Book of Deer* (London, 1994).

St Margaret and her historical context

L. Huneycutt, 'The Idea of the Perfect Princess: *The Life of St Margaret* in the Reign of Matilda II (1100–1118)', *Anglo-Norman Studies* 12 (1990), 81–97.

L. Huneycutt, *Matilda of Scotland: A Study in Medieval Queenship* (Woodbridge, 2003).

R. Oram, *The Canmores: Kings and Queens of the Scots 1040–1290* (Stroud, 2002).

R. Oram, *David I: The King who made Scotland* (Stroud, 2004).

R. Bartlett, ed. and trans., *The Miracles of Saint Æbbe of Coldingham and St Margaret of Scotland*, Oxford Medieval Texts (Oxford, 2003).

D. Baker, '"A Nursery of Saints": St Margaret of Scotland Reconsidered', in *Medieval Women*, ed. David Baker (Oxford, 1978), pp. 119–42.

D. McRoberts, *St Margaret Queen of Scotland* (Glasgow, 1957).

N. Hooper, 'Edgar the Ætheling: Anglo-Saxon Prince, Rebel and Crusader', *Anglo-Saxon England* 14 (1985), pp. 197–214.

M. Lapidge, J. Blair, S. Keynes, and D. G. Scragg, ed., *The Blackwell Encyclopaedia of Anglo-Saxon England* (Oxford, 1999).

Sources Cited

'The Life of St Margaret', printed in *Acta Sanctorum Junius II*, cols. 0320A–0340E (trans. Huneycutt, *Matilda*, pp. 161–78).

D. A. Bray, *A List of Motifs in the Lives of the Early Irish Saints* (Helsinki, 1992).

S. Keynes and M. Lapidge, *Alfred the Great: Asser's 'Life of King Alfred' and Other Contemporary Sources* (Harmondsworth, 1983).

Theobald of Étampes letter to Margaret of Scotland, ed. J.-P. Migne, *Patrologia Latina* 163, col. 765.

F. Barlow, ed. and trans., *The Life of King Edward who rests at Westminster*, Oxford Medieval Texts, 2nd edn (Oxford, 1992).

Goscelin, 'The Life and Miracles of St Laurence', printed in *Acta Sanctorum Februarius I*, cols. 0289B–0294E.

B. Colgrave and R. A. B. Mynors, ed. and trans., *Bede's Ecclesiastical History of the English People* (Oxford, 1969).

S. Keynes, facs. edn., *The Liber Vitae of the New Minster and Hyde Abbey Winchester: British Library Stowe 944 together with Leaves from British Library Cotton Vespasian A.VII and British Library Cotton Titus D.XXVII*, Early English Manuscripts in Facsimile 26 (Copenhagen, 1996).

G. Winstanley, *An Appeal to the House of Commons, Desiring their Answer...* (London, 1649).

H. Clover and M. Gibson, ed. and trans., *The Letters of Lanfranc, Archbishop of Canterbury* (Oxford, 1979).

S. Gwara and D. Porter, ed. and trans., *Anglo-Saxon Conversations: The Colloquies of Ælfric Bata* (Woodbridge, 1997).

A. H. Thompson, facs. edn., *Liber Vitae Ecclesiae Dunelmensis*, Surtees Society 136 (Durham, 1923).

H. Rackham, *et al.*, ed. and trans., *Pliny's Natural History*, Loeb Classical Library, 10 vols. (Cambridge, MA, 1938–62).

F. Wallis, trans., *Bede: The Reckoning of Time* (Liverpool, 1999).

S. Hollis, *et al.*, *Writing the Wilton Women: Goscelin's Legend of Edith and 'Liber confortatorius'* (Turnhout, 2004).

W. Stubbs, ed., *Chronica Magistri Rogeri de Houedene*, Rolls Series, 4 vols. (London, 1868–71).

G. W. S. Barrow, ed., *The Charters of King David I* (Woodbridge, 1999).

P. McGurk and J. Rosenthal, 'The Anglo-Saxon Gospelbooks of Judith, Countess of Flanders: Their Text, Make-up and Function', *Anglo-Saxon England* 24 (1995), 251–308.

C. P. Finlayson, facs. edn., *Celtic Psalter: Edinburgh University Library MS 56*, Umbrae codicum occidentalium 7 (Amsterdam, 1962).

B. Günzel, ed., *Ælfwine's Prayerbook London, British Library, Cotton Titus D. xxvi + xxvii*, Henry Bradshaw Society 108 (London, 1993).

C. Plummer, ed., *Two of the Saxon Chronicles Parallel*, 2 vols. (Oxford, 1892–9).

M. Swanton, trans., *The Anglo-Saxon Chronicle* (London, 1996).

G. P. Krapp, ed., *The Vercelli Book*, Anglo-Saxon Poetic Records II (New York, 1932).

S. A. J. Bradley, *Anglo-Saxon Poetry* (London, 1982).

R. A. B. Mynors, R. M. Thomson and M. Winterbottom, ed. and trans., *William of Malmesbury, Gesta regum Anglorum: The History of the English Kings*, Oxford Medieval Texts, 2 vols (Oxford, 1998–9).

P. McGurk, ed. and trans., *The Chronicle of John of Worcester III: the Annals from 1067 to 1140*, Oxford Medieval Texts (Oxford, 1998).

J. Raine, ed., *Reginaldi monachi Dunelmensis de admirandis Beati Cuthberti virtutibus*, Surtees Society 1 (London, 1835).

U. Lenker, *Die Westsächsische Evangelienversion und die Perikopenordnungen im angelsächsischen England* (Munich, 1997).

J. T. Fowler, *Extracts from the Account Rolls of Durham* (Durham, 1898), pp. 425–39.

D. C. Douglas and W. Greenaway, *English Historical Documents II: 1042–1189* (London, 1953).

Aelred of Rievaulx, *Genealogia regum Anglorum*, ed. J.-P. Migne, *Patrologia Latina* 195, col. 736.

Symeon of Durham, *Historia Regum*, ed. T. Arnold, *Symeonis monachi opera omnia*, Rolls Series 75, 2 vols. (London, 1882–1885); trans. J. Stephenson, *Simeon of Durham: A History of the Kings of England* (London, 1858).

R. Bartlett, ed. and trans., *The Miracles of Saint Æbbe of Coldingham and St Margaret of Scotland* (Oxford, 2003).

W. L. Leslie, *The idaea of a perfect princesse in the life of St. Margaret Queen of Scotland...* (Paris, 1661).